The
Backyard Bird
Chronicles

AMY TAN

The Backyard Bird Chronicles

Written and illustrated by

Amy Tan

ALFRED A. KNOPF New York

2024

THIS IS A BORZOI BOOK
PUBLISHED BY ALFRED A. KNOPF

Copyright © 2024 by Amy Tan
Foreword copyright © 2024 by David Allen Sibley

Library of Congress Cataloging-in-Publication Data
Names: Tan, Amy, author.
Title: The backyard bird chronicles / Amy Tan.
Description: First edition. | New York : Alfred A. Knopf, 2024.
Identifiers: LCCN 2023001929 | ISBN 9780593536131 (hardcover) |
ISBN 9780593536148 (ebook)
Subjects: LCSH: Tan, Amy. | Bird watching. | Birds. | Nature. |
LCGFT: Autobiographies. | Creative nonfiction.
Classification: LCC PS3570.A48 B33 2024 | DDC 813/.54
[B]—dc23/eng/20230123
LC record available at https://lccn.loc.gov/2023001929

Jacket illustrations by the author
Jacket design by Jenny Carrow

Manufactured in Italy
Published April 23, 2024
Reprinted Six Times
Eighth Printing, November 2024

FRONTISPIECE: Dark-eyed Junco (fledgling)

For Bernd Heinrich,
John Muir Laws,
and
Fiona Gillogly.

And, most of all,
to my dear editor, Daniel Halpern.
This book was entirely your idea,
and I am grateful beyond words for
reasons only you understand.

Anna's Hummingbird (female)

Foreword

by David Allen Sibley

When I was seven years old, on a bright and sunny spring day in southern California, a dozen or so male Yellow-headed Blackbirds were lined up along a wire, bold yellow and deep black against a bright blue sky. I tell people this is my earliest bird memory, but more precisely I should say it's my earliest "birding" memory, because I was already fascinated by birds. The spectacle of those Yellow-headed Blackbirds prompted my older brother to start keeping a "life list" (a tally of all the species of birds he saw), and weeks later that prompted me to start keeping a life list, too, and that transformed my interest in birds into a quest with a sense of purpose and even urgency. I never slowed down.

Like most kids, I enjoyed drawing and I laid down enough "pencil miles" (a fun phrase I just learned in this book) to develop some skills at a young age. So by the time my own bird obsession started to take hold, drawing was a natural part of that. I consider drawing mostly a brain exercise. The hand that controls the pencil to make lines on paper is a small part of the whole process. You can learn how to draw, and then drawing anything becomes easier, but drawing is really a different way of seeing, converting something from three dimensions in the real world to lines on a two-dimensional sheet of paper.

Drawing something, like birds, actually depends more on your knowledge of the subject than on your drawing ability. And it is a deep and intangible sort of knowledge. Imagine your very wise birding mentor saying, "Yes, it is black with a yellow head...but do you really *know* what that bird looks like?" Drawing requires you to absorb details and then to combine them into a simplified and unified whole. Watching birds for countless hours is the way to get to know them, and drawing is the test to demonstrate that knowledge. The drawing is, in a way, like discovering the birds anew, as they appear on your paper. It usually means testing lines and shapes, erasing, adding a curve, sharpening or softening an edge, working to find the details that re-create the essence of the bird in a drawing. And when that happens it feels like a small kernel of truth has been revealed.

I was lucky to be a bird-obsessed kid with an ornithologist for a father (which might not be purely a coincidence, of course). He was able to provide guidance, resources, and opportunities that are not available to most seven-year-olds, and I absorbed it all in the sponge-like way that kids do. My peers in birding were mainly adults, and by the time I was ten or eleven those adults were starting to ask *me* questions about birds—which is hugely empowering for a kid.

Birds made sense to me, a lot more sense than the tangled and ephemeral web of middle school alliances. So I just watched more birds. Even at that age, it was clear to me that everything about birds follows patterns. Every new detail that I learned could be tucked into some part of my growing network of knowledge, where it connected with other facts and created new patterns to build on. The patterns in birds are sort of blurry and sloppy, though, so birds manage to be predictable and surprising at the same time. Great Horned Owls have their habitual routines and favorite perches, so you can predict the best place and time to see one, but still, you will see a Great Horned Owl only on a small percentage of your visits. You can get to know the habits of Bewick's Wrens over many years, and then see one doing something completely different, like bathing in water. Hermit Warblers follow a broad pattern of migrating through the Coast Ranges of California at about the same time every spring and fall, but to actually see one in your own backyard during those periods is rare and unpredictable, and feels like a gift.

Like eclipses and comets, these rare bird events might come around only at very long intervals. Unlike astronomical events, however, the behavior of birds cannot be described by an equation. They appear where they choose to appear and do whatever makes sense to them at the time.

BIRDWATCHING IS much more popular now than when I was a kid, and birding's popularity surged even more during the COVID-19 pandemic of 2020. Many things have contributed to this rise. I think one of the biggest reasons for the decades-long increase in interest is a fundamental need to feel connected to the natural world.

In the last few generations our daily lives have become more isolated from natural rhythms. Climate-controlled buildings and electric lights allow us to keep the same schedule regardless of weather, seasons, or the time of sunrise and sunset. Refrigeration and other technology make almost any kind of food available at any time.

Only a few generations ago all of our ancestors were more connected to nature. They lived in houses, on farms, or in towns, not in wilderness, but life still moved to natural rhythms. Food was local and seasonal, and activities were planned around the daily cycle of the sun and the annual cycle of seasons. It was useful for them to know the birds by sight and by sound. The arrivals and departures of different species of birds were like a perpetual calendar, marking important dates in the changing seasons. Some birds were food, some were competitors (eating crops), some were helpers (eating pests that could destroy crops). In a way, everyone was a birdwatcher, as humans had been for tens of thousands of years.

The ability to recognize and remember patterns—one event or fact being associated with another—is a basic survival adaptation. Our brains have evolved to be very good at it, but it is a fundamental ability common to all animals. It's what allows a pet goldfish to anticipate when food is about to be dropped into its bowl. It allows birds to recognize that some people are dangerous, but they get fresh food when Amy Tan walks onto the deck. It allowed humans a thousand years ago to associate certain bird songs with the best time to plant crops. It allows birders today to identify birds, and to anticipate where and when each species can be found.

There are patterns everywhere, of course—for example, in regional styles of cooking or in the kinds of ads we see online—but I believe that we have a special affinity for the patterns of nature. The birds themselves provide an endless fascination of patterns—colors, shapes, sounds, movements, migration, nesting cycles, et cetera. Even more important, learning about birds opens a door to the entire natural world.

In the same way that having a friend in a distant city heightens our awareness of things that happen there, getting to know birds adds meaning and context to everything that is affecting their lives. We notice rain, wind, insects, frogs. We become attuned to plant communities—the countless variations of "woods" and "fields" and "mudflats," each preferred by different species of birds. We think about dinosaurs (the ancestors of birds), ice ages, ocean currents, continental drift, and evolution. We think about geography; even in a California backyard like Amy Tan's, it is possible to see birds that spend part of their year as far away as Alaska and Argentina.

Birdwatching is ostensibly about finding and identifying different species, and there is great satisfaction in learning the birds and how they fit together with one another and with their environment. But I think there is more. I think the most basic reason we enjoy birdwatching (and the same reason we enjoy other outdoor hobbies like gardening and fishing) is that it directs our attention outside, where we see the sunrise, feel cool mist or hot sun, watch an approaching storm, get bitten by mosquitoes, taste wild blackberries, and so on. It fulfills a deep and instinctive urge to plug into the rhythms of what is happening around us. It makes us part of something larger and gives us a sense of our place on earth.

ON THE SURFACE, this book is a nature journal; a collection of delightfully quirky, thoughtful, and personal observations of birds in sketches and words. Writing, like drawing, works best when it simplifies the complex, using just the essential words and phrases to show us the outline of a scene and convey an idea or a feeling, and Amy Tan, of course, is a master of that art. The drawings and essays in this book do a lot more than just describe the birds. They carry a sense of discovery through observation and drawing, suggest the layers of patterns in the natural world, and emphasize a deep personal connection between the watcher and the watched.

The birds that inhabit Amy Tan's backyard seem a lot like the characters in her novels. I can imagine this book being the notes for a new story with the cast of characters including the nonconformist Hermit Thrush, the comical towhee, the tiny but fearless hummingbird. Their lives intersect, diverge, collide. Some stay on the same few acres for their whole lives, raising families and enduring through changing seasons, floods, droughts, and predators. Others travel halfway across the globe to get there, trading the lean season for a daunting migration, with stories of loss and triumph, and a fierce and elegant determination to survive. It is a sweeping epic that spans generations and continents, and birds bring it to your backyard.

Identifying birds is just the beginning of birdwatching. Your wise mentor would say, "Yes, that is the name, but you must *know* the bird." Once you learn the names of the characters and start to appreciate their individual abilities and foibles, you realize that an infinitely expanding drama is unfolding in front of you. This book is really about getting to know the birds, learning their stories, and gaining a new appreciation of the world through that connection. As Amy writes in one entry: "Thanks to the birds, I have never felt cooped up staying at home. So much remains new, so much can be discovered ... when watching birds, I feel free."

Preface

These pages are a record of my obsession with birds. My use of the word *obsession* is not hyperbole. *The Backyard Bird Chronicles* contains excerpts from hundreds of pages gleaned from nine personal journals filled with sketches and handwritten notes of naive observations of birds in my backyard. I humorously titled the journals *The Backyard Bird Chronicles,* which delivers "breaking news," "new offerings," and "scientific discoveries." It began with simple observations of what the birds were doing in the backyard—eating, drinking, bathing, singing—in other words, what I thought were ordinary behaviors. My perception of those behaviors changed as I continued to watch day after day, year after year, most of the time as I was sitting at the dining table overlooking the patio, where I wrote my new novel, or tried to without leaping up whenever I saw a bird doing something I had never seen before, which was often.

The *Chronicles* is also a record of my growth as an artist. My love of drawing began when I was three, and by age seven, I secretly wanted to be an artist, although my career as neurosurgeon had already been predetermined by my parents when I was six. For many reasons, I gave up drawing, but my love of art continued through visits to museums, and occasionally I amused myself by drawing cartoons, among them the adventures of two male cockroaches who become deadbeat dads to millions of offspring. Early nature journaling at its best.

The *Chronicles* is also a record of my mindset as the "unreliable narrator" on behalf of my backyard birds. That is a term used in fiction writing to describe first-person narrators who are deceptive, unbalanced, or, in more benign cases, lacking in knowledge. The latter is me. When I started the *Chronicles,* I could recognize only three birds in my yard. What I did not lack was intense curiosity, and I have had that in abundance since childhood. That is also when my love of nature began. It was my refuge from family chaos.

BETWEEN THE AGES of eight and eleven, I lived in a suburban tract home a half block from a creek. In memory, the creek bank was steep and the water was barely more than a trickle that fed shallow ponds and temporary puddles. In that creek, I caught garter snakes. I grabbed lizards and sometimes was left with only their wagging tails in my hands. I watched the swarm of life in a splash of water the size of a cake pan, blobs that became polliwogs, or sometimes dead ones when the puddles dried up. I poked frogs to make them jump, ladybugs to make them fly, and pill bugs to make them roll into balls. I put a fuzzy caterpillar into a jar so I could watch it spin a cocoon and turn into a butterfly. I saw dismembered parts of animals and those covered in maggots, and I did not look away or cry.

Farther away from home, I sneaked into a cow pasture with squishy manure, fields that changed over the seasons, from fallow to a child's forest of corn stalks. I slid and tumbled down hillsides of dry grass in a cardboard box and bruised myself on jutting boulders. I sliced my calf squeezing between barbed wire on a fence with a No Trespassing sign that warned of prison. I climbed into the crook of a dead apple tree and when I slipped down out of control, a rusty nail gouged my knee deep into flesh. I never cried, and I still have that one-inch-diameter scar on the side of my knee, which I have unconsciously rubbed so often over the years I have made threadbare spots on many of my pants. The scar remains a badge of bravery and disobedience, a memento of my childhood when I made discoveries on my own, ones so exciting they overrode caution.

In that creek, I looked down, not up. That may be one reason I did not notice birds, except for big crows, which inspired no fondness. They looked like the murderous black birds in Hitchcock's film *The Birds*, filmed about twenty miles from where we lived. We kids were convinced that any black bird we saw was from the film. I vaguely recall that one attacked me. But that's likely a memory from imagination.

What remains of those three years are not just recollections of creatures I touched but the way I discovered strange wonders by crawling over shrubs, pushing aside brambles, crouching or lying on my stomach, slipping down creek banks, wading in water, and getting scratched up, banged up, or torn up. I sometimes do the same when looking for birds in the wild, all but trespassing. I ask for permission. Exploring that creek gave me joy similar to reading and drawing in the solitude of my room. It was pleasure without criticism, without the expectation it had to serve a future productive purpose. It was a refuge from the overwhelming craziness of a mother who often threatened to kill herself. I once ran away from home to go live in that creek, which became a brief stay when my mother offered me a tuna fish sandwich for lunch. Those three years in childhood ingrained not just my love of nature but my need for it.

In our college years, my husband, Lou, and I went backpacking in the backcountry of Yosemite, the only vacation we could afford. We followed stacked rocks that marked the trail, camped by lakes and rivers, and saw many coyotes, deer, raccoons, golden-mantled squirrels, the occasional marmot, and many bears, six of them on my first back-pack trip, who approached us at dusk. I caught a five-foot-long bull snake on one trip and took it home, which, in retrospect, was a bad thing to do. I found tarantulas and let them crawl up my arm, laughing as my companions ran off screaming. That's the kind of nature lover I am. Strange to say, in all my years of hiking and backpacking, I recall seeing only jays, crows, and turkey vultures who circled in the sky over dead animals. Nowadays, almost all our vacations are chosen to view wildlife—in the Galápagos, Botswana, Raja Ampat—or to examine life long extinct, like the dinosaur bones found at a dig in the Montana Hi-Line. This is to say that when I started nature journaling I was no city slicker who could not tell a Jeffrey Pine from a Christmas tree, poison oak from a hollyberry wreath. I loved being in nature. But before 2016, my explorations of nature did not include birds, and that now astonishes me. It did not include drawing them. It did not include watching them in my backyard.

I WAS SIXTY-FOUR when I took drawing classes for the first time, followed by nature journaling field trips, both led by John Muir Laws, "Jack," a well-known and beloved naturalist, artist, author, scientist, conservationist, and educator. I already had some of his guidebooks on birds, animals, and plants. After attending the first class, I bought his other books, *The Laws Guide to Nature Drawing and Journaling* and *The Laws Guide to Drawing Birds*. The classes were not strictly about drawing. If anything, they had just as much to do with being curious, allowing us to return to childhood wonderment, when everything was seen as new. That was the focus for beginning our drawings. To wonder in depth, to notice, to question. Among the many things I learned from Jack, and probably the most important to me, is this: "As you look at the bird, try to feel the life within it." For me that meant "Be the bird."

That came naturally to me as a fiction writer. To feel the life of the story, I always imagine I am the character I am creating.

Through Jack's classes and daily practice, I honed those skills to be utilitarian and specific, to be better able to represent the behavior of wild birds. That remains my focus. I still have much I want to learn how to do, like backgrounds as context and flying birds at takeoff and landing. Because I was still in a learning phase when I started *The Backyard Bird Chronicles,* the early pages show a general negligence about accuracy. Most of the sketches were done quickly, but had I known the journal would be published, I would have spent more time getting it right. Then again, I might have been paralyzed worrying that the drawings were all laughably flawed and would have devoted the rest of my life trying to make them perfect. As is, the feather structure I've drawn for a number of birds would have kept real ones land bound. From my not estimating the size of birds to the size of the page, tails and wings run off the edges or into the gutters. Jack provided classes on ways we might organize information, including placement of sketches, questions, our observations, and the date, time, and temperature. I remained disorganized. My pages might include the rough outlines of an animal, or a more detailed representation of one. The observations were captured in rambling notes with words squeezed at the edges of the page. The notes are written in slanted print or sometimes in near-illegible handwriting. There are misspellings, missing words, and wine or coffee stains. I now notice that a surprising number of my pages resemble comic strips. I gave the birds big cartoon eyes and bestowed them with the ability to make astute and humorous commentary on the situation at hand.

On field trips, we applied those lessons by sketching *en plein air* (fancy artist term for "outside, usually in a pretty place"). At lunch, we put our sketchbooks on a picnic table and shared what we had observed and drawn. I admit I suffered embarrassment the first time, when I saw that most people's pages were more interesting and better executed. That's because I tried to do a realistic rendition of one creature. I no longer remember what it was, only that it did not turn out well and was not about curiosity and wonderment. I did not add my sketchbook to the show-and-tell. We also posted our journal pages on the Facebook page for the Nature Journal Club, which Jack started. That required me to set aside perfection syndrome, which had plagued me all my life, especially as a writer. I posted my sketches, no matter how bad I thought they were. However, I did allow myself one accommodation to avoid self-consciousness. I took a pseudonym.

On the second field trip, I met a teenage girl, who had recently turned thirteen. She was accompanied by her mother. We were standing next to a wide body of water in the Consumnes River Preserve twenty miles south of Sacramento. Before us were waterfowl and wading birds. Sandhill cranes flew overhead, three thousand of them on their way to a nearby marsh field, outside of the town of Grove. Her journal pages were dense with fast watercolor sketches and question marks. *Why, how, what.* She asked some of her questions out loud to Jack or her mother. "I wonder why . . . ," she would begin. A child with endless unanswerable questions would be a challenge to be around—a nightmare, actually. I moved away. On the third field trip, I was with about twenty-five people following Jack through a fern grove. The annoying girl with the endless questions was in front of me, and every thirty or forty feet, she stopped to examine whatever caught her eye. She turned over a fern frond and pointed to rows of golden brown dots. "Sporangia spores," she said to her mother. "Fertile." I looked. So that's what those things on the back of ferns were, thousands of spores. She saw a manroot plant and traced it ten feet to where it started and ended. She saw birds in the distance. *Common Yellowthroat. Red-tailed Hawk, Ruby-crowned Kinglet.* I couldn't find them. I blamed the floaters in my eyes. She cocked her ear toward a tree and listened. "Hermit

Thrush. I love their song." Her curiosity and exuberance over so many things brought me back to that time in my childhood when I crouched and touched plants and animals, when I turned things over to see what was underneath, when I happily spent hours lost in curiosity and exploration, and was never satiated. I may not have asked endless questions aloud, but as a kid in nature, I wondered about everything.

On later field trips, I stalked her. I would stand close to her, and like a student cheating on an exam, my eyes darted over to see what she was sketching and writing. I asked her questions about the birds we saw, and she answered and also pointed out curious behaviors. That formerly annoying teenage girl is Fiona Gillogly, and her mother is Beth. Over the last six years, Fiona has been my nature journal mentor. Her name appears often in this journal. We see wildlife together and ask questions. In fact, in a few days we are going hunting for pellets—the indigestible parts of prey regurgitated by our resident Great Horned Owl. We'll dissect the pellets to examine the bones, teeth, vertebrae, and fur that are clues to what the owl feasted on. Fiona and I examine any dead animal we find and look for clues on how it died, which we then note in our forensic pages. We show each other what we've seen or found, and our questions spiral out. She embodies what Jack describes as "intentional curiosity," what leads us to deep observation and wonderment. Questions that beget more questions are the fertile spores that can lead you deeper into the forest.

From the beginning, I practiced drawing every day, putting in what Jack calls "pencil miles." Sometimes they were just shapes of heads or different neck lengths. I deliberately bought cheap sketchbooks so that I could draw freely, make mistakes, start over on the same page, without feeling I had wasted good paper. Unfortunately, the cheap paper in my sketchbooks was unfriendly to watercolors. Those pages buckled and formed murky pools or disintegrated. That's why there are almost no drawings done in watercolor. But the sketchbooks were fine for pencil, and that became the medium I found most satisfying, soft graphite, which skates over the page in a wonderfully sensual way and leaves smudgy fingerprints, evidence that I was absorbed in thoughts about nature. The messiest and most illegible are not among the pages here.

Early on, Jack advised we limit our supplies to get started, and to not overload ourselves with things we might never use. I should have at least tempered myself. I bought mechanical pencils in two gradations, .54B and .72B, ones that produced dark lines. I later added .3 HB and .9 HB. I then bought watercolors, gouache, ink pens that did not bleed, special kinds of erasers, blending sticks, pencil sharpeners, an embossing stylus, all kinds of pencil boxes, organizer kits, a crossbody bag, a spotting scope, a portable stool for drawing in the field, and my first decent pair of binoculars for $300, which, I have since discovered, would be considered low-end in cost by serious birders who spend thousands. They're good enough for this backyard birder. I tried colored pencils. They worked on cheap paper. I added fifteen Derwent waxy colored pencils in hues of nature, then twenty-four Prismacolors, thirty-six Verithins, forty-eight Polychromos, seventy-six Caran d'Ache Luminance, and a box of expensive pan pastels, which I ultimately decided were too messy to use. I also bought better sketchbooks, but they weren't better for the kind of drawings I did. I bought two antique tansu cabinets (at amazingly low prices) to hold the supplies that overflowed the cubbies, drawers, and shelves of my office. My husband and close friends know I am obsessive this way. (Twenty-three years ago, my love for my dogs led to my co-owning a show dog that became the number one Yorkshire terrier in the country and won breed at Westminster.) I know I will never use all those art supplies. But I was gleeful buying all of it. As a child, I had a couple of pencils, a stick of charcoal, and a few sheets of paper as my art supplies.

I soon experimented with my new equipment to do detailed drawings in pencil, and later, in colored pencil. They are not illustrations of species of birds. They are portraits of individuals who looked at me whenever I looked at them, who acknowledged and accepted me as part of their world. Doing the portraits was not the same as nature journaling. For one thing, they take anywhere from four to eight hours to finish. But doing a portrait had its own importance. Each of the thousands of strokes I made to create feathers became my meditation. I meditated on the life force within each bird I drew, about their intelligence and vulnerability. I once drew a fledgling Dark-eyed Junco who sat on a birdbath for twenty minutes calling for its parents. It had not learned to be fearful and wary of predators. As I drew the overlap of tiny feathers over its cheeks, I became that bird looking at me. If I could maintain the belief that I was the bird, I had a better chance of making the bird look alive, feel alive, present in the moment before I, the human, stepped outside to teach it how to stay alive. I shooed it away. By imagining I was that bird, I felt a personal connection to it and a deeper sense of what life is like for every bird: Each day is a chance to survive.

Because I cannot drive, Lou took me to the nature journal classes and field trips with Jack. But the field trips and classes happened only once a month. Had I been able to drive, I would have gone to parks, nature preserves, and "hotspots" listed in the eBird app. It took me a year before I realized I could do nature journaling in a place that was close by: my own backyard.

My backyard, it turns out, is a paradise for many birds. We built our house among four Pacific live oaks with overlapping canopies. They are eighty to ninety years old, and two of the geriatric ones have limbs that must be propped up. Some of the branches of neighboring oak trees overhang our patio, and up, down, and all around the immediate neighborhood are more oak trees. From roots to canopy, the oaks are the community hub for almost all the birds that either live here year-round or sojourn during winter migration. Asparagus ferns stand in the shade of the oaks and periwinkle vines creep around the trunks. For the fussy bird that wants variety, we offer a birch, a dogwood, a Japanese maple, and a lush nectar-bearing fuchsia shrub as big as a tree. Passion fruit, jasmine, ivy, and andromeda vines interlace the fences and elevated planter boxes. Four Meyer lemon trees and bushes of lavender, sage, and rosemary scent the sunnier areas of the garden, and nearby are fragrant roses, peonies, freesias, and narcissus. In the shadier areas of the garden, fern and orange lilies are lush, especially the lilies. During different seasons, the plants offer the birds clusters of seeds, berries, other kinds of fruit, as well as nectar for humming-birds and the occasional warbler. We tore out the lawn in the garden about twelve years ago to conserve water and created a succulent bed in a yin-yang pattern. Our roof garden was designed to offer a friendly habitat and food source for bees, butterflies, and birds. Seven types of flowering succulents bloom white, yellow, or pink flowers at different times of the year. I like to imagine birds using our colorful roof as the flyway sign to their fall migration getaway. Thanks to the birds, invasive plants always take root on the roof—oxalis, burr clover, Santa Margarita daisies, and coyote brush among them—their seeds deliv-ered by wind and in bird poop. Sprouted acorns on the roof, planted by Scrub Jays and squirrels, must be regularly dug out. If I were sell-ing this house to a bird, I would point out that water runoff from the green roof flows down rain chains with jingling bell cups, on which a little bird and its growing family can perch while drinking and enjoy-ing a view of San Francisco Bay.

My home is the backyard's complement, built to give the feeling of an open pavilion. Some have remarked that our home feels like an aerie in the treetops. Birds that have come into the house must have thought so, too. Two walls of bifold glass doors can be pushed all the way to each end, so that the room is open to a verandah on one side and a patio on the other. The glass doors next to the patio have hand-drawn white spider webs from top to bottom to prevent bird collisions. When standing on the verandah, I am at eye level with birds that are just below the oak canopy—titmice, chickadees, warblers, nuthatches. Depending on the season, I might see off in the distance pelicans, gulls, or cormorants flying over the bay. I can't tell what species because they are too far away. Even if I could identify them, I would not include them in the *Chronicles*. The shorebirds and water-birds that are plentiful along the Sausalito waterfront will always be NIMBY, Not In My Backyard. *The Backyard Bird Chronicles* has journalistic integrity and is true to its name.

Birders have described my yard as "very birdy." But it was not always that way. I had to lure these birds to check out my woodland habitat and make it so irresistible they would never leave. I first bought a feeder stand and hung from its arms a seed feeder and nectar feeder. That brought in a few new birds, and also the squirrels, crows and Scrub Jays. I then bought squirrel-proof seed feeders and discovered how smart squirrels truly are. I bought baffles and more highly touted squirrel-proof feeders, which brought out the athleticism of squirrels. I then went insane and built my own squirrel-proof cage feeders, which also kept out crows and Scrub Jays. I changed to hot pepper suet and seeds that the squirrels hated. I stored thousands of live mealworms in the fridge, without complaint from my husband. And this was just the beginning. My search for the right feeders and food became pathological. But I did find the most successful lure is also the cheapest: shallow saucers of fresh water for bathing and drinking. So that is the feeder setup that enables me to see the birds first thing in the morning when I am brushing my teeth in front of the bathroom window. At dusk, from the table facing the patio, I see hummingbirds taking their last sip of the day. And when dusk turns to darkness, I hear the Great Horned Owl sing before flying off for his nightly hunt.

Since 2016, I have gone from being able to identify three species in my backyard to now sixty-three, and no doubt more to come. A few are one-offs. Some spend the winter here before returning to Alaska or Canada. And many now live here year-round. So you know how birdy my yard truly is, it is December, and over the last two days my frequent visitors were six Oak Titmice, a pair of California Towhees, a Spotted Towhee, a Ruby-crowned Kinglet, a Hermit Thrush, two Fox Sparrows, passels of Pygmy Nuthatches and Chestnut-backed Chickadees, a Bewick's Wren, Mourning Doves, a whole bunch of House Finches and Lesser Goldfinches, a Purple Finch, many Dark-eyed Juncos, three Townsend's Warblers, an Orange-crowned Warbler, a Nuttall's Woodpecker, a couple dozen Golden-crowned Sparrows, a White-throated Sparrow, an American Robin, four California Scrub Jays, and a mob of American Crows that shriek at the resident Great Horned Owl. I know there are more birds high in the trees who have never visited the feeders. If I learn their birdsongs, I will know who they are. That's next.

CREATING THIS JOURNAL has been different from writing a novel. A novel is torment. It needs structure, tending of language, constant shaping, refinement, excision, and cumulative insights that might give it breath and breadth. I have to carry a thousand pieces in an increasingly complex configuration toward the luminous vision of a story that remains a mirage. I am driven to make each piece as perfect as I hope it can be, while making the story that is composed of those pieces feel spontaneous, effortless, and without gyre and gimble showing at the seams.

In contrast, creating *The Backyard Bird Chronicles* was pure fun, spontaneous, a bit of a mess, come what may. Perfection would have been the antithesis of spontaneity. There were no expectations. I could be openly naive and not self-critical. I could respect science and also allow playful anthropomorphism and a lot of wild guesses. Unlike fiction, I didn't need to hope the story pulled together. The story was the moment in front of me, one day, one page, one sketch.

Yet I also think my impulse to observe birds comes from the same one that led me to become a fiction writer. By disposition, I am an observer. I want to know why things happen. I need to feel the gut kick of strong emotions. I am drawn to see details, patterns, and aberrations that suggest a more interesting truth. I am obsessive and can spend months doing research that I may never use, but to me it is time well spent. For the birds, I have never stopped researching the best bird feeders and the most nutritious foods that will satisfy all the birds. There is always something else the birds would like more.

With both fiction and birds, I think about existence, the span of life, from conception to birth to survival to death to remembrance by others. I reflect on mortality, the strangeness of it, the inevitability. I do that daily, and not with dread, but with awareness that life contains ephemeral moments, which can be saved in words and images, there for pondering, for reviving the bird and my heart. With every novel I finish I think it's a miracle because three or four predecessors never came to life. With every adult bird I see, I think it's a miracle it is before me, because 75 percent of young songbirds die before the end of their first year. When I try to find the right image and words that capture an emotion, I must beat down clichés and homilies, which are devoid of fresh thought and honest contemplation. When I see a bird that has died, I don't accept the sanguine saying, "It's the circle of life." It is good to mourn and wish it weren't so.

As my gratitude and love for my backyard birds grow, so does fondness for these pages. The sketches and words are a record of my life.

They contain what puzzled me, thrilled me, what made me laugh and also grieve. They are like the scar on my knee when I was a child in nature. It contains my disobedience and bravery, my curiosity and discoveries, my pain and refusal to cry. In these words and drawings are what changed me when I was naive and curious and wondered about a bird I saw for the first time.

The
Backyard Bird
Chronicles

September 16, 2017

While watching hummingbirds buzz around me, I recalled a fantasy every child has: that I could win the trust of wild animals and they would willingly come to me. I imagined tiny avian helicopters dining on my palm. To lure them, I bought lilliputian hummingbird feeders, four for $10. Hope came cheap enough, but I was also realistic. It might take months to gain the hummingbird's interest in the feeder and for it to lose its fear of me.

Yesterday, I set a little feeder on the rail near the regular hummingbird feeders on the patio, and then sat at a table about ten feet away. Within minutes, a hummingbird came to inspect, a male with a flashing red head. He hovered, gave a cursory glance, and then left. At least he noticed it. A good beginning. Then he returned, inspected it again from different angles, and left. The third time, he did a little dance around the feeder, approached and stuck his bill in the hole and drank. I was astonished. That was fast. Other hummingbirds came, and they did their usual territorial display of chasing each other off, before the victor returned. Throughout the day, I noticed that the hummingbirds seemed to prefer the little feeder over the larger one. Why was that? Because it was new and they had to take turns in claiming it?

Today, at 1:30 p.m., I sat at the patio table again. It was quiet. I called the songbirds. Each day I pair my own whistled birdsong with tidbits of food to encourage them to come. In about two minutes, I heard the raspy chitter and squeak of the titmouse and chickadee. They sounded excited to find peanuts. Then I heard the staticky sound of a hummingbird. It was a male. I had left the feeder on the table where I was sitting. I put it on my palm and held it out. Within ten seconds the hummingbird came over, landed on my hand, and immediately started feeding. I held my breath and kept my hand with the feeder as

A Bird in the Hand

I had removed all the hummingbird feeds to clean and refill. While letting the nectar cool, I heard impatient hummers making crackling sounds. I came out with this hand feeder. Within minutes, a hummer came and did two test fly-bys, before dipping his bill into the nectar feeder, still beating his wings. It felt like a fan blowing on my palm. Then it landed and I felt its scratchy tiny feet. Two seconds later, the hummer and I were divebombed by another male, and my bird in the hand was gone in half a second.

It was enough. I am in LOVE.

SEPT 16, 2017
1:30 P.M.
SUNNY BUT WINDY

still as possible. His feet felt scratchy. He was assessing me the whole time he fed. We stared at each other, eye to eye.

I remembered what Jack Laws said: "Feel the bird. Be the bird." What did the hummingbird see in my eyes? Is that how a bird evaluates trustworthiness? As he fed, I examined the tiny feathers on his head, the pink, orange, and red color at his throat, the wing blur, the exquisitely tiny feet. I tried to mentally recite what I was seeing, so I could later draw the hummingbird: The overlay of tiny feathers on its head are successively larger as they move from the front of the bill toward the back of the head. The legs are short and its toes are the width of dental floss. What is he noting about me?

After a minute, the hummingbird shot up into the oak tree. He had remained on the hand feeder for forty-five seconds. Or maybe my excitement had lengthened the actual duration of that moment, one that altered my life. I had gained entry into a wild animal's world. It was my own backyard with a portal big enough for the bird I imagined myself to be. An hour later, I was seated at the patio table eating lunch when I heard the familiar sound of beating wings around my head. I am certain he was the same hummingbird, because when I held up the feeder he immediately settled and started feeding. After a minute, he flew up to my face, inches away, eye to eye. I could feel a little breeze coming off his wings. He seemed fearless, and I was slightly concerned his little sword would pierce my eye. Was he curious? Was he being aggressive, warning me that he owned the feeder? Whatever his meaning, he had come back. He had acknowledged me. We have a relationship. I am in love.

December 17, 2017

First thing in the morning, I always pull up the bathroom shades so I can see what the water looks like on the bay and harbor. It's different every day, sometimes flat and clear, flat and sparkly, gray and choppy. Whatever birds are on the feeders usually scatter as soon as I come to the window. Yesterday, one did not, a fluffy Pine Siskin. It continued to eat. A fearless bird, I thought, or maybe a newly arrived émigré, famished from the journey. I stepped out onto the porch. It was chilly. The Pine Siskin was still sitting on the bottom of the seed feeder, eating with gusto, just two feet away from where I stood. The puffed-up coat of feathers made me think it was a baby bird. I could see soft down peeking from under the larger spread of wing feathers. At times, the Pine Siskin stopped eating and closed its eyes. I guessed it was exhausted, a young bird getting its first meal away from the nest. But then I realized it was December, not spring. Would there be baby birds this time of year? Also, the Pine Siskins are migrants, not year-round residents. They do not breed here. I saw a mess gathering around its beak, the bits of sunflower seeds it had been trying to eat. Was it possibly sick? As if in answer, it abruptly flew to me and landed on my hand. It seemed dazed. This was bad. It hopped down to the water bowl and tried to drink. Water dribbled out of its messy mouth. It sipped more frantically before returning to the feeder. I noticed more. Its rump was soiled. It was shitting watery diarrhea. And then it sat motionless with its half-closed eyes.

I contacted U.S. Fish and Wildlife and learned there is a salmonellosis outbreak across the U.S. related to an irruption of Pine Siskins—meaning, a massive migration of larger than usual numbers. Because Pine Siskins gather in social groups, a single sick Pine Siskin could easily infect its tribe and any bird that visited the same feeders and water bowls it had used. From what I read, by the time a bird is puffed out and behaving strangely—like flying to a human—it would likely die within the day. I decided to catch the bird to take it out of circulation, keep it warm in a box, and take it to a wildlife rehab center, where if it could not be saved, it would be humanely euthanized. Although the siskin was slow, I missed catching it.

Today, I did not see the sick bird. It was probably dead. I've taken down the feeders. I gave away the bird food I had recently bought, sacks of sunflower seeds and Nyjer, blocks of suet. I am not sure I will ever use the feeders again.

I have been trying to do a drawing of the sick Pine Siskin, using as reference a photo I took before I realized it was sick. My attempts look flat and stiff. It's as if I've forgotten everything I learned about drawing birds. The joy is gone. In the photo, the signs of impending death are obvious. I now know too much about this disease. Its fluffed-out feathers were a futile attempt to stay warm because it could no longer thermoregulate. Its messy beak was due to an inability to swallow. Its half-closed eyes confirmed the ebbing of life.

To draw the Pine Siskin, I must work my way back to seeing it without heartache. I have to feel the bird is alive again.

Sick Pine Siskin

March 29, 2018

It's been nearly four months since I took the feeders down due to a disease that killed a Pine Siskin in my yard. I was lucky to see only one sick bird. Other bird lovers reported seeing many dead Pine Siskins every day. The epidemic finally appears to be over, and many bird organizations have said it is safe to put up feeders again. I bought sunflower seeds and refilled the feeders. No takers. After a couple of birdless days, Pine Siskins arrived. Because of my past heartbreak, I had hoped for juncos, titmice, chickadees, anything else. I am hesitant to give in to happiness.

The Pine Siskins are very messy eaters. I find all the finches are slobs. For every seed they eat, they reject four and toss them on the ground. I don't know the reason for this wasteful behavior, but their sloppy spillage makes the juncos very happy. Food conveniently delivered to the ground. The rats join in as clean-up crew, but they leave their shit behind in exchange.

Because the Pine Siskins stay at the feeder a long time, they are ideal subjects for drawing outdoors. In my case, *plein air* involves my standing barefoot at my bathroom window facing the porch to observe and sketch the birds. My first attempts are jittery. While they remain on a perch, they move their head a lot to check out their surroundings. I will have to practice much more before I have a gestalt understanding of Pine Siskins, let alone the other species of birds I hope to see. That would enable me to quickly draw the basic shape of the head, bill, and body, as well as the different postures. The direction of their eyes is crucial. They suggest the intent of their behavior. Right now, it's difficult to know where to place the eye when I am drawing the changing shape of the head from different angles. Look at this one— the top of the eye is higher than the beak . . . and now it is aligned in profile. Now it is looking right at me like a deer in the headlights. I am

Pine Siskin — caught with its mouth full

sunflower chips

messy eater

juncos eat bits on ground

toe grasp from below

auriculars more apparent

[?] juvenile — yellow bar on primaries faint. Very round and short

3.29.18

talking to myself as I draw the Pine Siskin eating its sunflower chips. In one of his nature journal classes, John Muir Laws advised we do this to encode the details into memory and understanding.

I sketch several head positions and must redo the eyes five or six times to make the bird look right—or rather *feel* right. I stop only because more attempts will tear a hole in the cheap paper and give the bird a hollow-eyed look. It has the proportions of what I imagine baby birds have—a relatively large head on a short round body. And that signature yellow stripe on the long primary feathers is quite faint. Then I remember, that like the Pine Siskin that died, they are migrants from the north that have their babies in their summer home, not this winter getaway. As I draw, I notice more. Its primary feathers appear to be very short, as is its tail, relative to the other birds on the feeder. How can it fly such long distances with those short wings? Or is that just my misperception based on the angle of the bird to me?

Why does that Pine Siskin keep staring at me? Oh, because I stared first? We are staring at each other as I draw its head and it eats seeds and makes a mess. It's not flying away. It's staying. Good. *Welcome back. I'm glad you're here.*

Pine Siskin

June 20, 2018

Alarm cheeps! Four newly hatched California Quail were wandering alone next to our garage. Marcia and the kids next door noticed them first. When we approached, they froze and quieted. One buried its head into the corner of the rock wall. If left out in the open, the chicks would be in danger of being killed by a cat, hawk, crow, jay, or car.

We figured the parents must be nearby. They live within bushes and bamboo hedges of a quadrant of houses, including ours. I see the covey occasionally in the yard, several blue males and about eight brown females. Is this a family or a harem? We placed the babies underneath a shrub and stood to the side to see what would happen. The quail adults came out immediately from a bush just ten feet away and sounded the urgent cry. *Ooo-OOO-oo! Ooo-OOOO-ooo! Kidnappers have stolen our children!* Soon four fluffballs raced out and joined their parents and a dozen other siblings. They moved quickly and smoothly together as a unit, as if on invisible roller skates.

I wonder how many of these chicks will survive. Unlike other birds, they are born capable of walking with those humongous feet, and they can peck the ground and forage. But they are still utterly defenseless. They cannot fly. Even adult quail are vulnerable because they are relatively slow flyers, no match against a hawk. Their best defense is subterfuge: to go under bushes and pretend to be inanimate objects. Babies, like the wandering four, are probably born with this instinct to freeze in place.

A quail's cry is always a message of great urgency. When I put millet on the bathroom ledge and flagstone, I imitate the alarm cry, *Ooo-OOO-oo! Ooo-OOOO-ooo!* It means they better hurry on over and eat up the millet before the Scrub Jay gets to it first. I don't tell them I will put out more if it does.

6·20·18

California Quail

1 day old.

← Topknot

Separated from mom + dad. They cheeped until humans came along. Then they became quiet and tucked into a corner.

July 10, 2018

The baby crows are somewhat smaller than their parents. But I can easily tell them apart by their blue eyes and constant crying and whining for food. They follow their parents, open their mouths as wide as bowls, and scream. The parents take them to my sunflower feeder, the one with a seed tube inside a wire bell-shaped cage, designed to exclude squirrels and any bird bigger than a sparrow. The inventors of this feeder underestimated the intelligence of both squirrels and crows.

The mother crow and her fledglings sit on the verandah rail facing the feeder. It is so close, yet, to a baby crow, so far. The mother demonstrates by leaping smoothly from the rail onto the feeder, grasping the wire cage with her feet. She looks at the fledges. *See how easy?* The cage is tilted downward with her weight, and seeds were knocked out when she landed. Then she returns to the rail, the feeder swaying slightly, and calls to the babies. You don't need a bird translator to know what she is saying: *Come on, you try it. Stop crying. I'm not going to feed you. Don't disgrace me.* One baby gets in position, crouching low on the rail. But upon launching, it misjudges the distance and height, and crashes into the feeder, which swings wildly as the baby flaps its wings to escape the monster. Sunflower seeds fly out. It lands with a wobble on the rail where its mother and siblings are sitting. The mother faces the baby and caws loudly. *Try again.* The baby's piteous cries sound like a higher-pitched version of hers, but more insistent. *I won't. I won't.* The mother squawks back again. The baby opens its mouth wide for her to feed it. The mother yells at it again, then flies off, leaving all the babies alone on the rail. Abandoned. Where's the love? They fly off to pursue their mother. I read that the parents of many species of birds usually stay with their fledglings for only two weeks. But crow offspring may remain with the clan for years, if not forever. Poor mom.

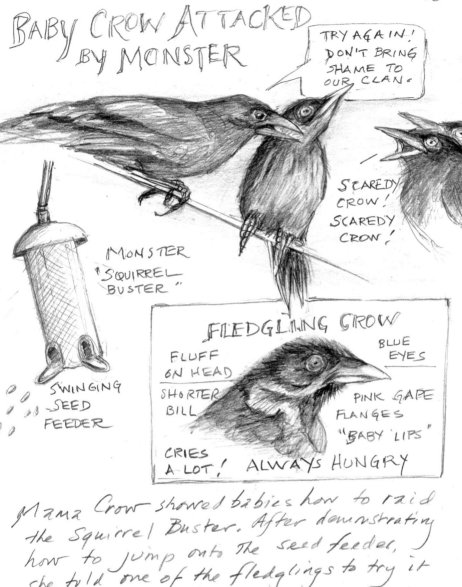

7·10·18

BABY CROW ATTACKED BY MONSTER

TRY AGAIN! DON'T BRING SHAME TO OUR CLAN.

SCAREDY CROW! SCAREDY CROW!

MONSTER "SQUIRREL BUSTER"

SWINGING SEED FEEDER

FLEDGLING CROW

FLUFF ON HEAD

BLUE EYES

SHORTER BILL

PINK GAPE FLANGES "BABY LIPS"

CRIES A LOT! ALWAYS HUNGRY

Mama Crow showed babies how to raid the Squirrel Buster. After demonstrating how to jump onto the seed feeder, she told one of the fledglings to try it out. The baby launched, missed, and refused to try again. She squawked, the baby squawked, and then abandoned the three babies.

July 10, 2018

Looking out my office window, I saw about a dozen crows on a flat top roof pecking for grit. I once thought birds ate grit because they were starving and would fill their belly with anything that was the equivalent of stone soup. Poor birds! Then an ornithologist told me that birds have to eat grit to aid in digestion. Oh.

One bird on the roof was much larger and I assumed it was an adult supervising this kindergarten of crows. I took photos from a distance. When I later looked at the photos, I was surprised to see that the larger one appeared to be a raven. I have heard ravens croaking like bullfrogs in our garden but had not seen them, whereas crows are frequent visitors. Was it possible that a raven was socializing with crows? Was that normal?

I then read that young ravens will gather in groups when they are learning to find food sources. When one is successful, the others come over to take advantage. Perhaps this was a young raven who had landed in a gathering of crows and was too young to discern by size or call that it did not belong.

But if it was a raven, wouldn't the crows gang up on it and drive it away? I've seen ravens do that to a huge Golden Eagle. Perhaps I am only thinking it is a raven because it's a wannabe bird, meaning, I want it to be a raven, a more unusual yard bird. I examine another photo. The bird looks like it has a canoe attached to a small skullcap. Its chest is shaggy and tattered. And the crow standing next to it is closer to the camera but a lot smaller. The big guy is a raven, no question, and maybe a juvenile in molt, too young to realize it had crashed baby crow kindergarten. The only lesson it would soon learn when the adult crows return is to stick to its own kind.

Kindergarten Crows ➡ or RAVENS?

Baby crows are being taught by their parents to hunt and peck — and raid our seed feeders. The babies cry when unsuccessful and the parents demonstrate.

About a dozen crows milled about on a nearby flat roof, learning how to find and eat grit, which aids in digestion.

JULY 10, 2018

In looking at photos, I was shocked to realize at least one was a RAVEN. The size of the bill, and body were distinctive. It was a dull grey brown and was clearly molting. But was it a baby raven socializing with crows?

Or was this the mother of a baby raven? Were they socializing with crows? Ravens are usually solitary or in pairs — except when babies are learning to find food. One bird is a raven. And the others are still a mystery.

August 18, 2018

I am pleased to see that my backyard has become a menagerie of fledglings—baby juncos, finches, and Scrub Jays—all learning to fly. Their goal is to land onto the patio cage feeders at an angle that enables them to enter via one of the 1½" grid openings. We're at baby steps. And some fledglings are slower learners than others. They hang on to the feeder. And to enter, they must swing up or let go to grab the grid bars closer to the top. A few remain stuck and cry for help.

Today, on the back porch, an adult Scrub Jay returned to its disconsolate baby sitting on the rail. It popped a seed into the crying baby's open mouth. They flew off together. She later brought it back to the feeder for another lesson. But the fledge balked and jumped down and ate fallen seeds on the ground instead. The adult flew off. Alone, the young bird walked upright to inspect the porch. It surprised me when it launched itself onto the feeder. *Where's Mom? She should see this.* Unfortunately, it remained hanging on to the bottom of the feeder, its tail tucked under, a position that made it unlikely it could hoist itself up. It was bug-eyed as it stared at the seeds so tantalizingly close. After fifteen seconds, it dropped off the feeder and made do with a few chips it managed to knock loose. I saw the baby jay an hour later, still trying to launch onto the feeder. It already shows a key trait of a very smart Scrub Jay. Persistence.

November 10, 2018

When I knew almost nothing about birds, I bought red hummingbird nectar in a bottle and a fancy hand-blown glass globe with a rubber stopper and spigot. I hung this on a shepherd's hook in an open area of the front yard. I never saw a hummingbird. I left the fancy feeder there, forgotten, for months. I later learned that feeders must be changed every few days, lest the nectar mold. The mold in my feeder was welded to the sides. The rubber spigot and stopper had cracked into pieces from being out in the sun. I also learned that store-bought red nectar is nothing more than water, sugar, red dye, and a waste of money. Better to make fresh nectar—one part white cane sugar to four parts boiling water. Skip the dye. Throw out the first batch of nectar I made with organic sugar. It's not better. It's bad for them. How many hummingbirds did I kill before I knew better? I trashed the fancy glass feeder, and later the charming replacements that were a pain in the ass to clean. I dumped feeders with metal bottoms that rusted.

I now have six acrylic feeders with clear bottoms and red lids. They're antithetical to the natural garden effect I wanted to create. I placed them in different areas of the patio, verandah, and back office porch. This afternoon I saw an Anna's Hummingbird approach one. Its head looked black until it turned toward light, and it instantly blazed iridescent red and pink. Reflected glory. It was a male. The females are a very classy subtle green with a few red spots at the throat. While aloft in a holding pattern, the male hummingbird did a quick surveillance of his surroundings, rotating his body and head in all directions to determine if competitors were nearby. Would he be the one who would chase or be chased? He delicately alighted on the feeder, wings still fluttering as his feet clasped onto the bar.

I've examined those tiny feet when hummingbirds land on the

NOV 10, 2018

BEFORE APROACHING, HE CHECKS TO SEE IF OTHERS ARE IN SIGHT. IF SO, HE WILL GIVE CHASE OR BE CHASED

THE MOTHERSHIP IS AHEAD — BECKONING WITH PROMISE OF NECTAR

ANNA's HUMMINGBIRDS at the FEEDER

BEFORE DRINKING, HE WAITS A SECOND OR TWO — COMPETITORS MIGHT COME TO CHASE HIM OR HE MAY CHASE THEM AWAY.

HOW DO THEY DECIDE? IS ONE ALREADY RECOGNIZED AS SUPREME?

HE DELICATELY ALIGHTS ONTO THE FEEDER, WINGS STILL FLUTTERING AS HIS FEET GRASP THE BAR.

palm of my hand to drink from a tiny feeder. Short legs, tiny feet, and teeny tiny toes and talons. They cannot hop, walk, scratch at dirt, or clutch food like other birds. Their toes can, however, grasp a wire, a spaghetti-sized twig, or the thin perch of a nectar feeder. And in battle with a competitor, they will aim those feet as a weapon. Are their feet that dangerous? Their talons on my palm feel scratchy, not lethal.

Today I discovered something else hummingbirds can do with their feet. A male hummingbird was chasing another, a female. The chase was leisurely, fond pursuit and not a chase. Season-wise, it seems late—or early—for courtship. Then again, I read hummingbirds can mate up to three or even four times a year. When the female landed on the limb of the oak tree, the male landed about two feet away and moved toward her. It was *sliding on his feet,* half an inch, half an inch, half an inch. When he was within ten inches, the female flew away. I swear he had the look of a jilted lover in disbelief. Was that indeed a courtship maneuver? Why didn't it land closer to the female from the start? Many animals draw closer to another to either gain affection or kill. Human teenagers in my day did that to flirt in a movie theater. *Oops, is that your leg? I was just reaching for more popcorn.* I read that among hummingbirds mating occurs when a female splays herself on a branch. So maybe this male was hoping the female would turn the branch into a nuptial bower right then and there. Sorry, bud.

The more I observe, the more I realize that every part of a bird and every behavior has a specific purpose, a reason, and individual meaning. Instinct does not account for everything that is fascinating.

Anna's Hummingbird (male)

November 17, 2018

It feels like the beginning of the end. The Camp Fire up north continues to rage after ten days. The smoke has drifted south to the Bay Area and to my backyard. I am conscious of the fact that this dirty air contains the remnants of what was once the town of Paradise, 176 miles away. Today in Sausalito, the air quality is rated 206, "very unhealthy." Elsewhere in the state, there are pockets where the air measures over 500, which is probably equivalent to smoking a pack of cigarettes every hour. I avoid going out, except to refill the bird feeders and change the water.

There are now only a few Anna's Hummingbirds in the yard. They may have fled south, but there are wildfires there, as well. Some left earlier, I think, because the neighbors whacked back the bamboo hedge, the hiding place for many birds. It was something that needed to be done; bamboo is a tinderbox for any wildfire. These days, when a hummingbird lands on a feeder, there are no male competitors to give chase.

I wonder how this polluted air is affecting wild birds. A friend who has pet birds said her favorite parrot died suddenly when it was exposed to kitchen smoke. Are wild birds equally sensitive? Are there stretches of fields and woods littered with beautiful birds that died of smoke-damaged lungs? If the birds did indeed leave because of smoke, I am seeing in real time how environmental change can rapidly cause a decline in bird populations, hopefully, in this case, only temporary.

Late in the afternoon, I was heartened to see a tiny Bewick's Wren, the same one, I think, that comes for suet several times a day, every day. I watch it eat, and it looks at me, the flightless creature who lives in a room with a HEPA filter that protects her from the hazardous air a tiny wren has to breathe. I worry.

WILDLIFE CHALLENGES

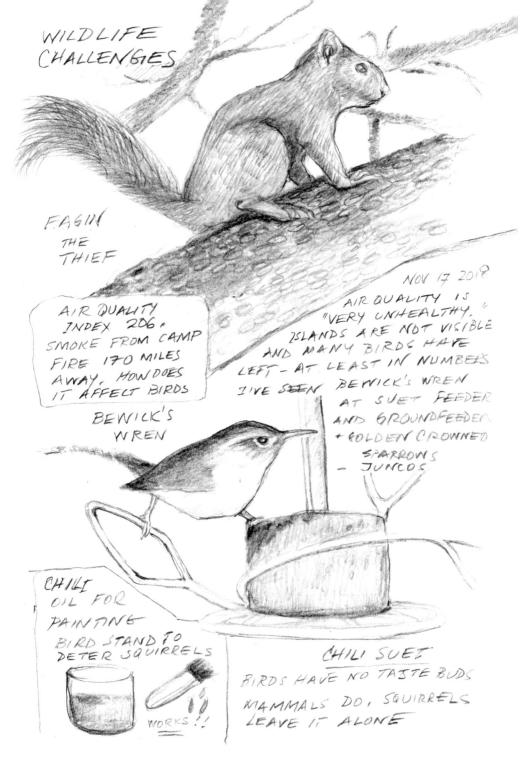

FAGIN THE THIEF

NOV 17 2018

AIR QUALITY INDEX 206. SMOKE FROM CAMP FIRE 170 MILES AWAY. HOW DOES IT AFFECT BIRDS

AIR QUALITY IS "VERY UNHEALTHY." ISLANDS ARE NOT VISIBLE AND MANY BIRDS HAVE LEFT — AT LEAST IN NUMBERS I'VE SEEN. BEWICK'S WREN AT SUET FEEDER AND GROUNDFEEDER + GOLDEN CROWNED SPARROWS — JUNCOS

BEWICK'S WREN

CHILI OIL FOR PAINTING BIRD STAND TO DETER SQUIRRELS

WORKS!!

CHILI SUET
BIRDS HAVE NO TASTE BUDS
MAMMALS DO, SQUIRRELS LEAVE IT ALONE

November 21, 2018

The finches are back in force today, and a food fight has broken out. I have front row seats at the bathroom window looking out onto the porch with feeders six feet away. Although the House Finches are much larger, the Lesser Goldfinches are more numerous and highly skilled at squabbling. As far as I can tell, the challenges often have to do with preferred perches at the seed feeder. Like some people, the finches want whatever other birds have, as if what others have is better than what they have. One Lesser Goldfinch occupied a perch at a seed feeder that a female House Finch wanted. There were several open perches. But no, the newcomer was insistent she had to have the one the Lesser Goldfinch had its little tush on. The House Finch loomed over the goldfinch. A stare-down. The Lesser Goldfinch maintained its position. The female House Finch arched her back. Meanwhile, a male House Finch sat on a perch at the same feeder, watching and munching sunflower chips, as if he were at a sports bar. Eventually, the Lesser Goldfinch went to the other side of the feeder, and that shift enabled the two to achieve detente. Who knows for how long?

Why did the Lesser Goldfinch hold out against a larger competitor? Beyond the House Finch's fierce stare and arched back, what are the other aggressive traits I am not aware of? Do they raise feathers slightly, like a hissing cat? Do they have an equivalent to a frown? Do they exhibit tension that only a bird recognizes? And how do they signal intention to attack? So much in bird communication and body language flies right over my head.

Not that long ago, I would have described what was happening in simpler terms: birds come and go. Now standing still, I am watching them and they are watching me, and we see each other hiding in plain sight.

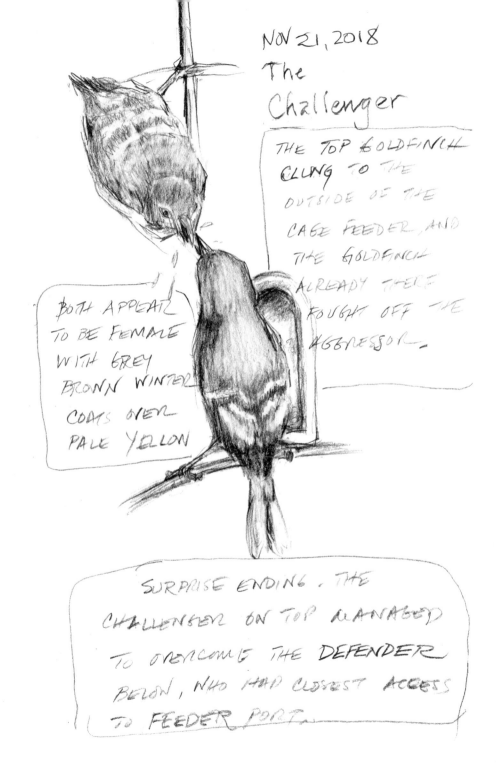

NOV 21, 2018
The
Challenger

THE TOP GOLDFINCH
CLUNG TO THE
OUTSIDE OF THE
CAGE FEEDER, AND
THE GOLDFINCH
ALREADY THERE
FOUGHT OFF THE
AGGRESSOR.

BOTH APPEAR
TO BE FEMALE
WITH GREY
BROWN WINTER
COATS OVER
PALE YELLOW

SURPRISE ENDING. THE
CHALLENGER ON TOP MANAGED
TO OVERCOME THE DEFENDER
BELOW, WHO HAD CLOSEST ACCESS
TO FEEDER PORT.

December 3, 2018

When I first saw this tiny bird on the suet feeder a couple of months ago, I experienced what I call "New Bird Tachycardia," palpitations from the excitement of spotting a species that I have never before seen in my yard. I thought perhaps this would be a one-time visitor, and to capture it in my mind, I followed Jack Laws's technique of saying aloud the most prominent features, its behavior and the situation. *"Neon yellow and black head, beak is warbler style, body as small as a chickadee, black mask, dull olive back, some yellow on body. On the verandah suet feeder. Jabbing action. Omigod! It's looking at me. Displeased expression. Sorry…"* I then quickly made a rough drawing, so I would not forget. I found a possible match on iBird. Townsend's Warbler, a brightly colored male. Within the hour, the warbler returned, and I confirmed the ID. I wished a fellow birder was there so I could brag over a bird I believed would be a rare one-off.

The Townsend's Warblers are regular customers now. I think there are four of them, three males and one female. They squabble over rights to particular feeders. Their rules: Only one warbler per feeder. And a dominant male warbler will displace another that is already there. I am always glad to see them. Often, they are the first birds I see at the feeders in the morning—on the back porch, by the bathroom window, on the verandah, and on the patio. I don't get up at the crack of dawn, so they likely come much earlier than I realize. Because they eat all day long, I see them whenever I look out the window. What are the warblers doing with all that food? It would not be for nestlings. They breed up north in the spring. Are they caching it for the winter? Hey, Warbler, there's a lot more where that came from, every day, every hour. No need to save it for a rainy day. I'm a dependable human. Every bird says so.

This warbler makes repeated trips to the suet — 5 times an hour. He is usually a termite eater, but evidently will go to a feeder if the goods are tasty. Since he eats so often, what does he do with all that food — cache it for the winter? The oak titmouse takes one suet ball per visit and returns to the tree.

vivid yellow and black make it easy to I.D.

TOWNSEND'S WARBLER
DEC 3, 2018

December 18, 2018

I put suet out two summers ago with high hopes I'd draw an instant crowd. I believed the hype on the packages. *All birds love suet.* I found few takers, except for crows and Scrub Jays. A friend told me the reason for my suet failure. Songbirds eat suet only in the winter, and only certain birds like it. I did not question her, and indeed it seemed to be true. I reasoned that songbirds avoid it because, like me, they find it a greasy, lethargy-inducing meal—fat, grain, insects, and peanuts. Last December, I tried again. I put suet in a couple of the cages. The suet went untouched for a week or so. But then some of the birds discovered it, and the chirps went out, and ever since, nearly all the birds flock to it year-round: the Townsend's Warbler, Bewick's Wren, White-throated Sparrow, California Towhee, Scrub Jay, Mourning Doves, almost all of the regulars.

Maybe the suet I was putting out this time was better quality, the Wild Birds Unlimited brand. I have become a mother who wants her birds to eat only the best, no GMO, no artificial flavorings or cheap cracked corn. My birds know nothing about my good intentions. They peck at it and eat what crumbles off. The chickadees, juncos, and titmice prefer taking the mini suet balls up to the trees, and the juncos eat crumbs of suet on the ground. The only birds that don't eat suet are the hummingbirds and the finches. It's odd to me that none of the finches will touch it, not the House Finch, the Lesser Goldfinch, or the Pine Siskin. They are seed and thistle eaters, and don't seem to deviate from that, not even for mealworms as a pigs-in-a-blanket kind of appetizer. They eat seeds, nuts, and berries, a vegan diet. Hey, I eat a vegan diet, too. Now I understand. I, too, wouldn't touch pork fat and insect antennae.

Unfortunately, the squirrels love the suet, too. I tried all kinds of methods to keep them out. I bought cage feeders with small open-

ings. The squirrels either chewed through the plastic bits or jumped on the feeders to set them swinging, scattering seeds out of the ports. Cone baffles kept them from climbing poles, but the squirrels would leap onto feeders six feet from tree branches, the fence, or a railing. They're like Olympic gymnasts with grappling hooks for feet and an ingenious criminal mind.

But now I've finally found the solution. Hot Pepper Suet, also from Wild Birds Unlimited. I accidentally touched my eye after handling the stuff and thought I was going to be forever blind. Inferno-strength stuff. And here's the proof: The squirrels no longer raid the feeders. They don't even bother to come by for a sentimental look-see. The birds, on the other hand, aren't bothered by the hot pepper at all. I was told that birds have no taste buds. I later read that birds can indeed smell and taste, but not enough to be bothered by spicy food. Who knows, maybe they find the chili-infused suet tastes better than the brand with lower-quality insect heads. Review of Amy's Bistro: *Sichuan offerings. Highly recommend.*

Western Gray Squirrel

December 23, 2018

Breaking news from *The Backyard Bird Chronicles*. At 2 p.m. I saw large flocks of crows flying over the patio from different directions. There were about ten to twenty in each cawing cloud. They took refuge in the oak trees nearest the patio. Others landed on our green roof where they scanned the sky and screamed. A few dug up and ate the caches of food on the roof that the Scrub Jays and squirrels had hidden. The songbirds dispersed when the crows flew nearby. Later most of the little birds returned and remained at the feeders on the patio. They must have concluded the crows were not interested in their food and were not a threat. But the crows remained alarmed about something. I guessed the reason: Some terrible person had murdered a crow in broad daylight.

Okay, I admit I placed the dummy crow hanging upside down on the rail next to the patio. Our yard was becoming a crow hangout, which scared the other birds. They were making a mess, knocking the feeders every which way to shake out seeds. I bought the dummy crow from the bird store. It was a little small for a crow, but it was well-proportioned and covered in black chicken feathers, some of which were askew, giving the impression that a mighty battle had taken place before the valiant crow succumbed to the murderous human. Crows are smart, so I was impressed that a $14 fake crow had so easily fooled them.

I wonder if the crows were mourning their fallen member. Given so many had flown in from all directions to join the mourning (or lynch mob), the fake crow must have resembled a much-loved muckity-muck member of the tribe. Would they mourn a crow they didn't know? Humans do. I have, for the victims of 9/11, for children shot in schools, for fictional characters no less real than a fake crow.

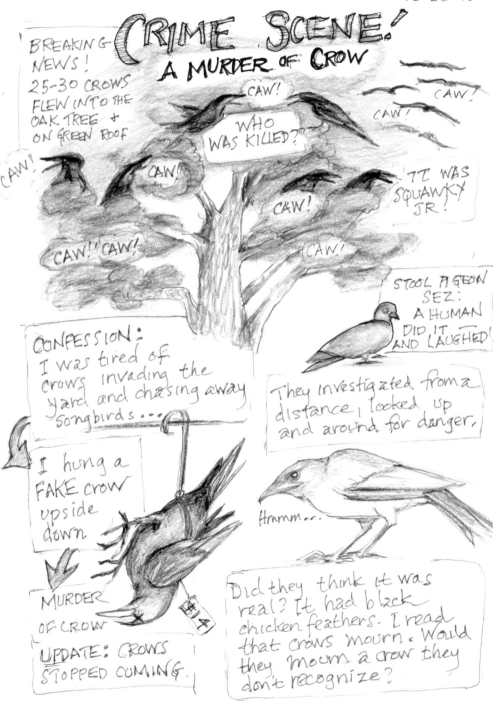

December 27, 2018

Through reading *The Genius of Birds* by Jennifer Ackerman, I have at last found the answer to my questions about how birds sing and what they sing. To summarize Ackerman, birds have a syrinx deep in the chest. It consists of cartilage and two membranes that vibrate against each other with air flow. Muscles of the syrinx can push that flow very precisely and this vibration produces songs and calls ranging from raspy sounds to complex melodic sounds varying in length and variety. No other creature has a vocal mechanism that comes close to producing such a variety of sounds and songs, even dual sounds in harmony.

This is exciting knowledge to me because I have long wondered how an Anna's Hummingbird makes its sounds. I read that its courtship dive and loud chirp-pop at the end was the result of air pushing through the hollow rods of the outer tail feathers. I then thought the clicks and staticky buzzy sounds they make might also be mechanical and related to forced air—until I took video of a male hummingbird visiting a nectar feeder. The hummingbird approached, took a quick drink, then moved backward. He did this about ten times, all the while making staticky clicking sounds. I then recorded it in slow motion. When it moved forward, it made two soft sounds in rhythm with a tail swing. The sounds in the slowed video sound vocalic, not mechanical, like an echoing bellow from a whale's song. Each vocalization almost always accompanied the tail swing, a sound forward and a sound backward. Sometimes it made no sounds with the tail swing, and sometimes it made sounds while holding still in an upright position. But most often, the pattern was sound and motion together. The swinging motion no doubt served as propulsion and brakes. But did tail swing also create a bellows effect that increased air pushed through the syrinx? I was reminded of the grunts that burly weight-

Vocalic Sounds and Motion in an Anna's Hummingbird
SLOW MOTION RESEARCH

hovering before pressing on the feeder

tail in a neutral position

SOFT GROANS!! with tail bending

Bends thrusts tail upward Tail fans out

Tail still tucked and fanned out.

moves back, away from feeder.

preparing to approach the feeder. Body is almost horizontal. Grunts again when tail moves.

SOFT GROANS when tail swings straight and tight

QUESTION:
Is the movement of the tail like bellows tho — push air over the SYRINX. Remind me of weight lifters who groan loudly in the gym. Vocalic and mechanical?

DISCOVERIES IN SLOW MOTION
I took video at regular speed watching Anna's moving toward the feeder. I heard clicking sounds and wondered if they were mechanical I slowed the video to 25 seconds. The "tick" was actually a groan, soft like a whale call, very vocalic. Each time the tail bent upward or downward it moved forward or backward, and the groan was part of the tail movement. It was not 100% correlation — It made the groan on one occasion when hovering in place.

lifters make when doing bench presses, which to my ears sound like straining of the bowels when constipated.

What is the reason for these rhythmic sounds in motion? Maybe it is related to courtship and the male hummingbird is vocalizing about the strength of its tail. Or perhaps it is the equivalent of a human singing, "I've been working on the railroad," in sync with nail pounding. Do female hummingbirds make the same kinds of sounds? Are they higher-pitched? Somewhere in the ornithological literature, there must be a simple answer—or not, as I am frequently reminded. Birds are not at all simple. They do what is beyond my ken, what I can only imagine, unless science or reincarnation enables me to become a bird.

12·27·18

WHY and HOW
do ANNA's HUMMINGBIRDS MAKE THOSE CLICKING SOUNDS?

I MADE FRESH NECTAR !!

CLICK! 'M CLICK!

GOOGLE TRANSLATE
" Get away from my food, or I will poke your eyes out! "

Clicked when approaching.

No clicking while drinking from feeder in my hand.

QUESTION

Is the clicking vocalic or mechanical, meaning produced by syrinx, or by pushing air through tail shaft, as with the deep courtship dive & pop?

Today, a hummer approached me with bill open - It was clicking and it either vocalic or made with tongue clicks.

CLICK! CLICK! CLICK! CLICK! CLICK!

I STAND STILL, EYE TO EYE.

ME: HE DOES NOT LIKE ME. ←

PATTERN: Fast clicking ensues when I or another hummer is close to feeder it claimed. Chases away hummers. But one time approached me and was close to my face. FANNED OUT TAIL!

OMG!   BEAT WINGS LOUDLY + CIRCLED MY HEAD.

December 28, 2018

I put out a pile of sunflower chips on the patio for the ground feeders. Soon, two nearly identical-looking Golden-crowned Sparrows approached by pecking at seeds on the periphery. But when one moved in closer, the other, a smaller sparrow, pounced in lunging hops and chased away the miscreant. Eventually the chastened bird returned and cautiously ate along the perimeter on the opposite side of where the other bird was feeding.

I am curious whether the behavior might be a dominance ritual; one bird chases away a competitor, and the other returns in a subservient position. Was the smaller bird a female and the other a juvenile from her brood? Was it older? A breeding bird? Or maybe the smaller bird was simply in a foul mood. Just because they're birds, I should not deny that they too have good days and bad. Some of the birds always act pissed off, like the male hummingbirds.

The other puzzle: Why do they eat only from the periphery and not from the center of the pile? Pigeons, I think, would go right for the glut. I do notice that ground feeders, like these sparrows, as well as juncos and towhees, will peck at random seeds on the patio, even though there is plenty of food still in the cage feeders they just exited. My non-scientific guess: They are ground feeders and by their nature and honed by necessity, they peck wherever there might be food. One solitary seed is as valuable as one in a pile. There is also the possibility of getting pecked by another bird who has already claimed the pile and is waiting to see what fool does not know that. There are no rules of politeness when a tiny bird can starve in twenty-four hours.

SEED ECONOMICS
or
RESOURCE GUARDING
among
GOLDEN-CROWNED SPARROWS

They were eating seeds on the patio, but only from the periphery of the pile. The smaller bird (female?) advanced in lunging hops on the other. He retreated and she took over seeds from his side.

slightly smaller - is it a female?

same pale coloration

The bigger GCSP eventually returned but ate at the farther edge of the pile.

- why was the female more dominant? older? Mother?
- why do they eat from the edge and not from the center?

slightly larger - male?

December 30, 2018

Odd observation: Female Anna's Hummingbirds seem to come more often to a feeder when I am standing next to it. It seems I am their bodyguard from males who would otherwise chase them away. Is that why I haven't seen that many females before? The males must have been aggressively keeping them away from the feeders, and thus the females chose to get nectar from the flowers in the yard. In the spring, many kinds of birds hang out in the old fuchsia shrub. It's ideal for little birds that need to hide. The boughs are laden with nectar-rich pink panicles. That's where I've seen many female hummers. No fast food for them. But now it's winter and today a female hummingbird chased a male away from the porch feeder and returned victorious. She sipped for well over a minute. I saw a female at another patio feeder this afternoon sipping without interruption. Is it just one female who is doing this? Or is a suffragist movement taking place? Is this the start of the nesting season?

The nectar feeders now run nearly empty every few days. Before, they would be half-full when I cleaned them. I fear the hummers are stocking up and will soon depart. They did that last year, even though they are supposedly year-round residents. Or are the females stocking up on energy reserves because they will soon be nesting? Something is happening. Something is going to happen. Oh, how I wish for the pitter-patter of teeny tiny feet, the blur and breeze of soft baby wingbeats.

ANNA'S HUMMINGBIRD FEMALE

12·30·18

Recently, I've seen more females. They even chase males away from the feeder.

How often do they feed at the nectar feeder?

Will some leave? They did last year.

FEEDERS are emptying quickly. But they don't migrate.

Once they land, they will remain on the feeder for a minute or more if undisturbed. They are certainly not perturbed by me. Instead, they often fly to the feeder when I arrive. Do I discourage competitors by my presence? What reason would they have to come when I am there.

January 10, 2019

The Lesser Goldfinches and House Finches are always fighting for a toehold on a small window feeder that can hold only two birds. I, the good human, found a new and improved feeder for them. I used the bottom half of a round hummingbird feeder to create one big enough to hold six birds. I took away the old and hung up the new.

The finches do not appreciate my thoughtfulness or ingenuity. They sit on the edge of the improvised seed feeder, seemingly puzzled over the disappearance of the smaller one. There is a bounty of seeds right beneath their tiny talons. How long before they figure it out? If one bird has the *aha* moment, will the others quickly learn from its discovery? Meanwhile, chickadees, juncos, and Golden-crowned Sparrows are sitting in the camellia bush staring at the empty spot of window, in position to jump up as soon as the old feeder returns. That's my interpretation. Maybe they're just staring at me, pissed that I took away their favorite eatery.

I've discovered that when birds have been successful in finding food in a certain location, they don't immediately give up looking for it. Last week, when I moved the suet feeder about a foot to the other side of the stand, a Townsend's Warbler kept returning to the former location, and would not visit the feeder in its new location. So, I moved the suet feeder back and, sure enough, the warbler returned. The hummingbirds are quicker to drink from relocated nectar feeders, but they will still check out the old spot. It's as if they see the feeder in a new location as a completely new feeder, and the other is simply missing. Somehow this feels familiar. I've done that before, seeing something old as new.

Birds are creatures of habit in their habitat. Me, too.

JAN 10, 2019

MISSING BISTROT

CREATURES OF HABIT AND HABITAT

The bistrot was here this morning

LESSER GOLDFINCH

Damn lying squirrels

HOUSE FINCH

CHEZ HUMMINGBIRD

I replaced a broken window feeder with a repurposed hummingbird feeder. The finches looked for the old feeder and then sat on the new feeder, never noticing the sunflower seeds. They left. They returned and were curious but cautious about the feeder. By the end of the day, the new feeder was mobbed. I find birds have the same reaction if I change the food, even I replace seeds with mealworms — their favorites. Habit of memory.

January 30, 2019

In 2016, when I first started paying attention to birds in my backyard, I loved the rascally California Scrub Jay. Along with the crows and hummingbirds, they were the first birds I could identify, although I did mistakenly call them "Blue Jays," the eastern species of jays. The Scrubbies were easy to spot by size and their vivid blue coloring. Flashy, brassy, sassy. They came often and demolished the sunflower seeds in the suspended copper feeder. That was gratifying to see. I was so new to birdwatching back then that I bought sunflower seeds in the shell. Note to self: *Shelled sunflower seeds* does not mean the seeds have been shelled. Those shells were left in messy piles on my back porch and on the ground next to the camellia bush. Apparently, the Scrub Jays also dropped a number of intact shelled sunflower seeds. Or maybe they deliberately buried them, as they are wont to do with acorns. Sunflowers sprouted, grew tall, and before I could harvest the seeds, the Scrub Jays ate them fresh off the flower head. Farmer Jays! Another lovable behavior.

Then I heard that Scrub Jays eat songbird eggs and hatchlings. Perhaps that was not often, but it still disturbed me. By then, I had many songbirds coming to the yard. I aimed my binoculars and could see many little eyes and wings and feet. I could identify the birds. I got rid of the open copper feeder and bought cage feeders that the jays could not get into, hoping that would discourage them from coming around the yard so often. But that just made them smarter in looking for ways to break in. Caw-caws went out into the Scrub Jay community that the human had put up challenging IQ puzzles. Mensa members of the neighborhood Chess Club for Scrubs came to my yard for laughs. *Har, har har, yet another flightless human who thinks she's smarter than a corvid.*

JAN 30, 2019

CALIFORNIA
SCRUB-
JAY

I have to be
grateful to the
Scrub-jay.

The Scrub was
the first bird   I could
identify, besides   the crow.
Both are corvids and their
raspy calls competed with each
other for "most likely to disturb the
peace in the garden." They are large
compared to the songbirds, although
the juveniles are rather short in
body. Often they are comical
in efforts to steal seed.

January 31, 2019

The male Anna's Hummingbird has become my favorite bird for a simple reason: They trust me. They tolerate me, seem curious. When I sing a lousy version of their song, *chur-rhee chh-chh*, they soon answer back and will then come to me and stare or even feed from my hand. For a while, six or seven of them visited the feeders at least ten times an hour. But when I returned from a two-week trip, they were absent. I refilled the feeders and sang their song. A lone female came a few times, but later she left whenever she saw me.

Their temporary disappearance is puzzling. If it is avoidance, that is sad and I need to know the reason. They had been courting just before I left town. I know that Anna's Hummingbirds do not mate for life. In a single season, each male may mate with several females. Had the males in my yard succeeded in winning over all their chosen females? Did they leave to mate with unclaimed females elsewhere? Even if that is the case, that would not explain the disappearance of the females. Are they brooding already? Do they come out only when no one is looking so as not to divulge the location of their babies?

I have never seen a hummingbird's nest. Nor have I seen a hummingbird carrying materials to build a nest. I know they never use bird houses, not to nest, rest, eat, or have clandestine love affairs. Those kitschy miniature bird houses marketed as hummingbird love nests are a scam, but people buy them because it gives them hope they might see a hummingbird and her babies. What's wrong with hope? I also know that hummingbirds use sticky spider webs to bind together a strong flexible nest that attaches like rubber cement to a branch and expands as the babies grow. I never remove spider webs in the yard, nor from my windows. I look at the webs and say to myself: *A baby hummingbird might need this to stay alive.* Besides, I love spiders. I love

THE RETURN of the MALE HUMMINGBIRD

JAN 31, 2019

Females are timid. They consistently cower, leading me to believe They are nesting here.

Two weeks ago, the male hummingbirds disappeared from the feeders. I called and there was no answer at dawn or dusk — primetime feeding times. A lone female showed up and she was easily scared by my presence. Eventually, I saw other females on the other side of the house, but no males, I was bereft because the males' familiarity with me had translated into anthromorphism as friendship and understanding based on trust and respect.

MALES are polyandrous — multiple females

Today, a male arrived and then another, there was no territorial fighting. Perhaps this behavior reflects the nesting season. The males have already won over females and can live peaceably for now. Is this typical? Males are polyandrous. Did the go elsewhere to find more females?

watching the orb weavers spin their webs and later encase their prey into an arachnid's version of Fly Wellington.

So where would a hummingbird nest in my yard? In the bamboo hedge? Up high in the oaks? In the camellia bush right in front of my bathroom window? Both male and female hummingbirds hang out there a lot. Or did. A friend said that she has a hummingbird that regularly nests in her potted ficus plant on the patio, forcing her to tiptoe quietly when she wants to lounge in the sun. Those are Southern California hummingbirds, very casual about nests and other people's property.

And now I've just read that Anna's Hummingbirds can have up to three or four clutches in a year if food resources are good. So many chances to see a nest! They also start mating and building nests in January, meaning now. From rereading Bernd Heinrich's *The Nesting Season,* I learned that female birds may not produce eggs immediately after mating. They cache the sperm and build the nest first. When the nest is ready, they release ovum to be fertilized with the cached sperm. Such a smart system. Like an in-vitro fertilization clinic, but a lot cheaper.

I continued to see more shy females, but no males—until now. The first male remained on the feeder as I approached. Then I saw another, a smaller, less colorful male. It, too, remained. They were too colorful to be babies. Was it possible these were males that had been here before? I want to believe that, and I would love them even more for their loyalty. But, of course, their return has nothing to do with loyalty to me. They're coming back to a sure thing—females and food.

I still like my anthropomorphic explanation the best. They left because I left. And now I am back and so are they.

February 15, 2019

I noticed that a lone Lesser Goldfinch sitting on a seed feeder did not move when I came out onto the patio. I had a bad feeling as I approached. Its eyes were nearly swollen shut. A pain shot through my heart. Conjunctivitis. It's a disease more common among finches in the wild, and not just at the feeders. I now had a terrible responsibility: to remove the seed feeders that the finches love so much. Usually there are 15–20 finches that visit at one time, and these birds would run the risk of getting infected by this sick goldfinch.

Before taking down the seed feeders, I tried to catch the sick bird with a butterfly net so I could take it to the local wildlife rehab center WildCare. Conjunctivitis is not a fatal disease. But it can be a fatal condition. If the bird is temporarily blinded, it cannot find food, and by sitting out in the open, it is an easy target for hawks. I was too hesitant with the net, and the bird, while nearly blind, was able to fly to a nearby tree. The goldfinch will later return to this spot and find nothing to eat. Being blind, it will be at a loss to find food elsewhere.

The next day, the finches flew back and forth to different areas of the patio and nearby bushes. They seemed frantic, desperate to find the food. I watched from the bathroom window. A few of the birds went right up to the window and stared at me. *Did she eat it herself?* A Lesser Goldfinch and a Purple Finch, which I rarely see, tapped the window with their bills. Were those taps really intended for me? "Feed me," they seemed to be mouthing with their moving beaks. Did they really associate my human form in a window as the source of their food? In the past, when food was plentiful, they flew off whenever they saw me approach. Now that the food is absent, they seem to be acknowledging that I am connected to their source. The following day, all the finches were gone. The tapping at the window stopped.

The porch where they gathered became a bird ghost town. I hoped they could find seeds in the wild. Spring comes early here.

I disinfected all the empty seed feeders. I will wait a couple of weeks before putting them back up. But I did not take down the suet feeders in other areas of the yard. None of the finches have ever gone to those, and the other birds count on suet at Amy's Winter Resort: the Townsend's Warblers, the Downy and Nuttall's Woodpeckers, the Dark-eyed Juncos, Bewick's Wrens, Chestnut-backed Chickadees, and Oak Titmice. Sure, they can forage for food the old-fashioned way, prying bark to get to creepy-crawlies. But then why stay at Amy's Resort?

It's been raining hard, and the suet feeders are now under the covered porch. Crowds of birds come before and after each downpour. I still see in my mind's eye the goldfinch with its swollen eyes. Did it fly off with the others? Is it sitting alone on the branch? I imagine it making futile forays to this now empty spot it knows by the habit ingrained by a precise number of wingbeats. I see it in my mind sitting on a nearby branch, wet, starved, weakening until it falls to the ground, dead. Such heartbreak comes with love and imagination.

YOO HOO!

I'M STARVING!

TAP! TAP!

Lesser Goldfinch can't believe the feeders are gone. She taps the window when she sees me. So, she recognizes me as the purveyor of food?

LESSER GOLDFINCH

HEARTBREAK at my window! I BECOME A CRUEL HUMAN.

YOU RARELY SEE ME!

HEY! IT'S ME — PURPLE FINCH

THE SITUATION: I discovered a Lesser Goldfinch with conjunctivitis. I removed the seed feeders. Congregating birds can spread disease.

YOU ONCE LOVED ME!

TAP! TAP!

The finches came to the window next to where the feeders. They stared at me. They tapped the window with beaks.

They don't understand they could go blind.

April 29, 2019

Just three weeks ago, I was taking much pride in my yard's popularity. Over thirty species of birds had been spending at least part of the fall and winter in my yard. I kept track of their IDs. The birds sang their many versions of courtship songs. As I walked up the front steps, I was serenaded by the orchestra of life. But then the birds abandoned the feeders and yard en masse. Rejected! Why? Those beloved birds have become foul-weather friends. They took advantage of me, gorged on my expensive store-bought food, then dropped me like bird shit.

A birder friend tried to console me saying their departure is not unusual during the nesting season when they go off bower-building elsewhere. What's wrong with my backyard as a nursery? Another birder said it was because record rainfall had finally created a profusion of blooms, insects, and butterflies. There were greener pastures and I should not take offense. But I, too, have a garden of flowers, bushes, and trees. I have a blooming living roof.

I try to find other reasons to not feel personally rejected. Our trees are populated by squirrels, crows, and Scrub Jays, which are known to eat eggs and hatchlings. Perhaps the songbirds do not consider our yard a safe place to raise a family. But every tree in the neighborhood has those.

I can still hear the birds calling and singing in the distance. The loud police whistle refrain of the Bewick's Wren's song sails over the others, making it sound like it is only a treetop away when it is probably several yards distant. I dislike these unknown neighbors with their caviar of seeds, fabulous blooms, and profusion of berries. Do they serve bigger organic mealworms? Do they have an Italian fountain with a statue of Buddha?

This afternoon, I heard the nearby raspy call of a pair of Spot-

4.29.19

Spotted Towhee

THE 2018-19 WINTER BROUGHT
AT LEAST 30 SPECIES TO MY YARD. THEY
SANG LOUDLY IN THE TREES. BUT INEXPLICABLY
THEY LEFT EN MASSE. THE FEEDERS ARE
FULL BUT ABANDONED. THE MEALWORMS WRITHING
UNEATEN. I SEE SQUIRRELS, CROWS & SCRUB
JAYS. I HEAR BEWICK'S WRENS. AND
THEN I HEARD THE RASPY CALL OF A SPOTTED
TOWHEE. ANOTHER ANSWERED. THEY FLEW
TO MY YARD.

ted Towhees, beckoning each other. They were somewhere on the other side of the patio fence. They sounded like they were challenging each other in hoarse voices: *"Eh?!" "Eh?!"* I called back, *"Eh?!"* A Spotted Towhee immediately flew over the fence and stared daggers at me with its orange eyes. At last, a bird I can see, the male, a beautiful bird with a black-hooded head, white-spotted black wings and orange sides. It hopped into the low planter and out of view, back to its mate. If it believed I was a challenger for its mate, then my ability to speak birdese must not be as bad as I thought. Then again, maybe it was insulted that I was doing a parody as insulting to me as someone imitating my Shanghainese mother scolding me as a child: *Eh?! Eh?!*

I am going to start learning bird songs. I will lure them back by singing off-key. They will return to see what lousy singers have taken over the home and mealworms they abandoned.

May 4, 2019

I am on high alert! I saw a song sparrow gathering dried grass before going into a clump of flowering plants by the side of a house. My heart went into a clutch. Two neighborhood cats have been stalking birds at the nearby feeders and I know baby birds could be among their victims. I read that between one and two billion birds are killed each year by cats. Unfathomable. I now saw those outdoor cats as serial killers. I got out the hose, and the cats sped away before they could get doused.

On Facebook, I've read posts by cat owners who say that it is cruel to keep a cat indoors, and that it is a cat's wild nature to roam outdoors and hunt. I am tempted to reply: Domestic cats are not tigers. There are cat owners who say their cats are outside for only a few hours a day. I want to reply: Cats do not have off-hours when hunting. I have also heard some cat owners rationalize that it is okay to leave cats outside if they have bells on their collars. I should explain: That does not deter a cat that eats flightless hatchlings in nests on the ground. But I do not reply because that would result in a hissy, yowling name-calling cat fight. It would change no minds, only cause deeper entrenchment of views. I'll just have to haze any cats I see. Yell. Aim the garden hose. Sic the hilariously small dog on them.

In the 1970s, I used to be one of those unconcerned cat owners. I had an irascible feral cat named Sagwa whom I loved for twenty-one years. My feral cat was indeed wild in nature, born outdoors on a rainy night. Her file at the vet clinic was marked DANGEROUS in two-inch high letters. Back then, I would have ranked my cat's pleasure in sunning herself as far more important than a bird's mutilation. She went in and out using her cat door for thirteen years, until I made her a completely indoor cat to keep her from getting injured in cat fights. She was missing one of her best defenses: her claws, which I clipped weekly, to save, not birds, but my sofa from getting shredded. When she became terminally ill, we closed off her cat door, and she never cried to go out. She was content lying in the window box perch we installed. From there, she oversaw the backyard—for the next eight years. We also tuned in to a TV program she loved, *Wild Kingdom*. When the lion spotted a porcupine and crept down low, she did too. When the lion sprang for the kill, she leapt. And when the lion roared in pain, covered with quills, she ran off in fright. Cat owners should play videos of birds so their cats have the thrill of the bloodless chase.

Each day I look at the birds and they look at me. Each individual bird is different. Each individual has its personality. What if owners of roaming cats noticed their backyard birds looking at them? What if they saw the same bird looking at them day after day? What would they then feel if they witnessed it suffering as their cat played with it as a live stuffed animal? Maybe the owners would no longer thank their cat for the lovely bouquet of loose feathers. It's not too late for them to become besotted with birds, to rejoice over their presence and mourn their unnecessary demise.

MAY 4, 2019.

"FAGIN"

SQUIRREL
Puzzle solver, hard
worker, undeterred

It's not just
raptors, wind
turbines, cars,
window strikes,
poisoned rodents
and hunters that
kill birds.
    Squirrels, rats,
blue jays, crows,
cowbirds and others
eat eggs and nestlings.

1
ROGUE =
OUTDOOR
CATS

"Miss Havisham"

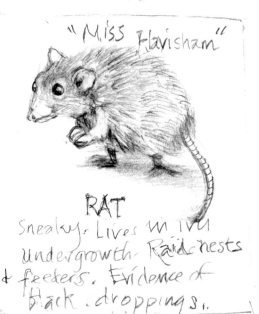

RAT
Sneaky. Lives in the
undergrowth. Raid nests
& feeders. Evidence of
black droppings.

May 6, 2019

Whenever a bird stuffs itself silly and also grabs a beakful of food to go, I suspect it is feeding either nestlings or the female who is brooding the nest. I have been watching this Oak Titmouse going to town on a bowl of mini suet balls, the perfect little delivery package for babies. The balls contain fat, insects, peanuts, and grain, the same stuff as the suet cones. They are easy to carry in a small beak, and there is no need to break up the suet into smaller pieces. It is already soft enough for a baby's delicate crop.

I've sensed for a while that birds develop food habits and are puzzled by any change, for example, when their feeder is relocated, switched out, or supplied with different food. To test that idea once again, I switched out the little suet balls in the titmouse's favorite feeder to mealworms. I was told by seasoned birders that all birds love live mealworms.

The mealworms are not really worms, not those annelids that tunnel into dirt. They are beetle larvae, on their way to becoming pupae and, soon after, inedible black beetles. I got a thousand of them at Wild Birds Unlimited. They are about an inch long and have a somewhat stiff toasty orange exoskeleton, and tiny bristling legs. The nine-year-old boy next door thinks they are cool and picks up fistfuls with his bare hands. I use nitrile gloves to put them in the bowl that once held the little suet balls.

The titmouse stared at the bowl. It searched the perimeter of the cage. It looked at the bowl again, then flew to another feeder. Again, no tiny suet balls. It returned to its once-dependable favorite bowl and stared at the mass of wiggling food. It gingerly picked up a mealworm but dropped it as soon as the weird thing contorted. After a short pause, the titmouse picked up another and put the wiggler under its foot, as it does with sunflower seeds, and hammered away at it. When

the mealworm was good and dead, the titmouse took his bounty to the nearby oak tree. The female and her babies must have gone crazy over this newly slaughtered food, because the titmouse immediately returned many times over the next hour, and it didn't bother to kill the food before taking it to the nest. At one point, the titmouse came once every thirty seconds. But then I wondered if I was seeing two titmice, the male and the female, taking turns in procuring the takeout food for their voracious babies. The adult would swallow four to six mealworms, then carry back another three or four in its bill. I will not know how many nestlings they have been feeding. But to judge by how many mealworms are being consumed, there have to be at least four.

Bernd Heinrich has a pretty good estimate of the amount of food nestlings can take in. He found featherless sapsucker nestlings that had been killed falling out of their nest. The stomachs contained half their weight in ants. The more food that is available, the better the chances are that all the nestlings will survive, unless they fall out of the nest.

I have my mission. Shell out more money for more live mealworms. Get over the disgust I feel when they writhe in my gloved hand. Pity them just a little as I place them into storage containers and then into the fridge so they don't change into pupae and beetles. Imagine the excited faces of baby birds oohing and cooing over what mama and papa brought them. Thanks to me for buying them are not necessary.

May 16, 2019

I am controlled by birds. I have been feeding these birds live meal-worms, 700–800 squirmy beetle larvae a day! I estimate this is costing me about $250 a month. Each week, it takes at least an hour to sort out the worms and get them into the fridge. How many fledglings and adults are there in my trees? I am told the Oak Titmouse fledglings look like adult birds but would still have the residual "baby lips," a.k.a. the fleshy pink or yellow flanges that enable them to open their mouths as wide as foot-pedal trash cans. Since the titmouse is territorial, can more than one nesting pair occupy an oak tree? I have five oaks, plus other smaller trees. And the neighbors all have oak trees, some of which overlap our yard. Can birds of different species, like the Chestnut-backed Chickadee, occupy the same tree?

Three titmice are now coming at the same time. One goes in; the others sit on top of a pole and wait their turn. Two parent titmice might feed cooperatively. But three adults? Maybe I am seeing two parents and one fledgling. Or perhaps it is one adult with two fledglings. But where are the yellow baby lips? Even with binoculars, I can't see them. Whatever the case, they have to compete with the Scrub Jay that chases off all the songbirds. Then the crow chases off the Scrub Jay, and I reign supreme and chase off the crow. As for the squirrels, Bobo, my personal rat patrol Yorkie, is in charge of those, and he sends them scrambling over the fence, where they will wait until he goes back into the house. This is all part of the gentle semicircle of life. No one gets eaten.

I love the mornings when I step out and all is quiet. As soon as I whistle, the birds call out—not singing prettily, but loudly calling. They hop from branch to branch, and I can tell where they are by the flickering movement of leaves. Those calls come from different sets of titmice, nuthatches, chickadees, and Bewick's Wrens. Are they signaling my presence as a danger? Or could it possibly be they recognize I am the patron saint of very expensive mealworms? Yes, that's what it means, to judge by the three Pygmy Nuthatches standing on top of the fence. An impatient one flits down to a nearby feeder, clinging to the side, watching me carefully as I dole out the mealworms. More birds come and propagate like Christmas ornaments on a wispy tree. They are crying out to their clan that it's chow time. They are shrieking for me to hurry up and get out of the way. It's the noisy start of a new day.

5-16-19

THE HUNGRY MORNING CHORUS

Pygmy
Nuthatch

Bewick's
Wren

Oak
Titmouse

Chestnut-
backed
Chickadee

They sing for
their supper—
morning,
noon,
night,
dawn,
dusk,
before it
rains,
after it
rains.

How many are in
the oak trees? Are
they coming back for
seconds and thirds, or
are there large numbers
waiting their turn.

June 16, 2019

A surreptitious pair of California Quail flew up onto the office porch and looked about, inspecting the surroundings, as if they were potential buyers of a new home. *Good location for sun, but in need of some better hideouts, more shrubs here, rocks there.* They settled in and were soon furiously pecking at dropped seeds—until four-pound Bobo, ever alert to lurking rats, and now rotund quails, barked his head off as he stood by the glass door. I am impressed by how slowly yet effortlessly the quails glide up to a branch of the oak tree—their ponderous bodies rising like helium balloons, the little flag on their crowns waving farewell.

I can see the female on a bough, preening. Her coloring is a lovely brown spackled over her back and breast. Her belly is covered with triangles of white that resemble coconut shavings from a distance. With binoculars, I can see those white feathers are laid out as precisely as interleaved pineapple skin. The more colorful male is behind oak foliage. I toss out more seed onto the porch patio. They will wait until I leave. They are experts at remaining as still as rocks for ten minutes or longer before they approach the food and throw caution to the wind, the same wind that hawks float on looking for bird food, especially the bobble-headed quails. I throw more seed out to make sure the quail see it. And then I make myself as still as a rock.

CALIFORNIA QUAIL 6·16·19

They are in the bamboo hedge and do not often fly to feed. a pair came to the porch to munch on dropped seed bits...

Guard dog BOBO flew up to an oak branch. The female preened.

When the MALE took off so did the female

DROPPED SEED BITS

June 19, 2019

At dusk, an obese rat crawled out of the thick ivy under-brush next door and squeezed through the fence opening. I watched it move across the patio in nervous spurts. Two more rats, much smaller ones, remained at the far edge of the patio, close to the planters of asparagus ferns. I guessed they were rodent youngsters, and the fat one was their mother demonstrating valuable life skills of subterfuge and thievery. The rat's goal is to eat as much expensive bird food as possible. My goal is to stop the rats from coming onto the patio, and to succeed without killing them.

When I switched out the regular sunflower chips and suet for the hot pepper version, the squirrels took one bite and abandoned the feeders entirely. The rats, however, continued to eat the bird food. Today I upped my game in two ways. I added an extra sprinkling of ghost pepper powder, the kind given to game show contestants who attempt to eat the hottest peppers on earth without calling an ambulance. To add to the challenge, I created the Rube Goldberg of rat-deterrent cages. I put the enhanced suet in a square bowl that hung in a bottomless cage feeder. I placed the cage feeder on top of an empty three-foot-tall ceramic planter with upwardly sloped, slippery sides. A rat would have great difficulty climbing up to reach the feeder. Even if it could, to reach the suet, it would have to lean against the sus-pended blue bowl, and that would cause the bowl to swing, and the rat would then lose its balance and fall into the dark depths of the unknown. Although the rat could climb up the rough interior sides with great effort, a neophobic rat might look down at the abyss and reconsider. And all rats are indeed neophobic. That's why they avoid all those newly invented rat traps.

A junco sat on top of another cage feeder and watched the rat. Do birds experience something akin to spectator amusement? The rat

6.19.19

The Night Stalker : BLACK RAT

Comes to feeders
at dusk

8 inches
not including
tail

I always know it's there. The dogs
go crazy.

All the
food is
in cages
that it can't
enter.

It can't
reach the
food. The
seed
droppings
are chili-
coated. But
it does not give up.

Poops
alot!
Diseases!

Live and let live? There is a rat catcher
in the neighborhood. It leaves feces the
size of our dogs' poop. Is it the fox?

looked up at the feeder on the ceramic planter. It did not try climbing the slippery sides. It leapt up, no problem—shit!—then grabbed the bars of the cage and looked at the hanging feeder just out of reach. Minutes passed, and I was about to declare victory when, in a split-second blur, the rat somehow sprang into the cage, grabbed a huge chunk of suet, and jumped to the ground, leaving the bowl swinging wildly. The rat furiously chowed down, as her kids watched from the side. Suddenly, the rat shot up as if electrocuted, and ran up the rock wall. Its reaction reminded me of naive diners at a Japanese restaurant who slather onto their maki a dollop of wasabi, as if it were butter, then jump up from their seats, gasping for a fire extinguisher. The extra pepper dusting had done the trick. No more rat raids. But after a few seconds, the fat rat returned and resumed eating the fiery suet it had dropped. I chased it off but it managed to take the chunk of suet with it. The rat kids have now learned a valuable life lesson: Never give up. You can adapt to anything, be it a heap of rotting garbage in a land-fill or tricky bird feeders laced with 100 megahertz chili suet in the lovely garden of a writer. Rats are excellent promoters for extermination companies. They are never defeated, only momentarily deterred. There will always be a need for someone to invent a better rat trap.

I have sympathy for rats, but I still dislike them. They are unlike domesticated pet rats that can show affection. They carry diseases that can sicken the dogs. Leptospirosis. Parasites. They leave shit behind to let you know they have been everywhere. They scurry and dart like thieves. And they can breed starting at nine weeks of age and can produce litters seven times a year. That last factoid is the beginning of a horror movie. Fortunately, the lifespan of rats in the wild is only about a year, a reflection of the unsanitary and hard conditions in which they live. So how do I keep them from coming? Poison is out of the question, of course. I saw a rat slowly crawl across our walkway once. Someone had poisoned it. Its body was hideously distorted, its lungs heaving for air as the gardener came down with a shovel to put it out of its misery. Hawks, owls, and other animals could die from eating a poisoned rat like that. And I would never use torturous methods like glue traps. I tried a catch-and-release trap, but succeeded in catching and releasing only sheepish-looking squirrels back into the yard. I later learned that releasing rats in unfamiliar terrain without burrows and their social network dooms them to a slow death by starvation and exposure to the elements. It seems the only thing I can do is sweep up the mess left by the birds on the patio, verandah, and porch. Every day I sweep and sweep and sweep—the birds are so messy. I sweep and hope the rats will capture the interest of our other clandestine visitors—the Cooper's Hawk, the Red-shouldered Hawk, and the Great Horned Owl. Or how about the gorgeous fox that sometimes strolls through the yard on a midnight ramble? The rats can serve a noble purpose as needed sustenance. Let nature take its first course.

June 30, 2019

I've been spending more hours a day staring at birds than writing. How can I not? Just outside my office, four fledgling Scrub Jays are learning survival skills. They are comically unskilled in balancing on whatever perch they find to reach food.

One landed on the flimsy branch of a camellia bush facing my bathroom window. The branch bent low under its weight, until the young bird lost its balance, which caused the branch to fling the young jay up into fluttery flight. Another landed on a fern frond, which collapsed into the middle of the plant. A third landed on the curved top of a wood post and promptly lost its grip and slid down the metal stair rail. Two flew into bushes while chasing each other and got their wings tangled in the tiny-leaved branches. Another wobbled while atop a shepherd's hook and then slipped rapidly downward and nearly crashed into the feeder before it jumped off. Yet another landed on a small perch, then leaned over to the feeder's opening, and succeeded in grabbing a seed, before losing its balance and its hold on the seed. The fledgling looked down to see where the seed had fallen. Another young jay that had already positioned itself below the feeder was already eating the seed.

Yesterday, I put dead mealworms in a pan and set it at the bottom of the stairs of my office porch. They died, unfortunately, in the heat, and unlike the dried mealworms that still looked like mealworms, these had turned black and smelled bad. The songbirds would not eat them. The young jays, however, flocked to the pan and engaged in a food fight. When one baby jay took a dead mealworm, one of its siblings flew toward it with a dramatic show of flapping wings and squawks. Usually that ploy works. But it seems that the young jays are not that good at defending their stash, and are better at being the aggressor. One sneaked up from behind its sibling and clamped its bill

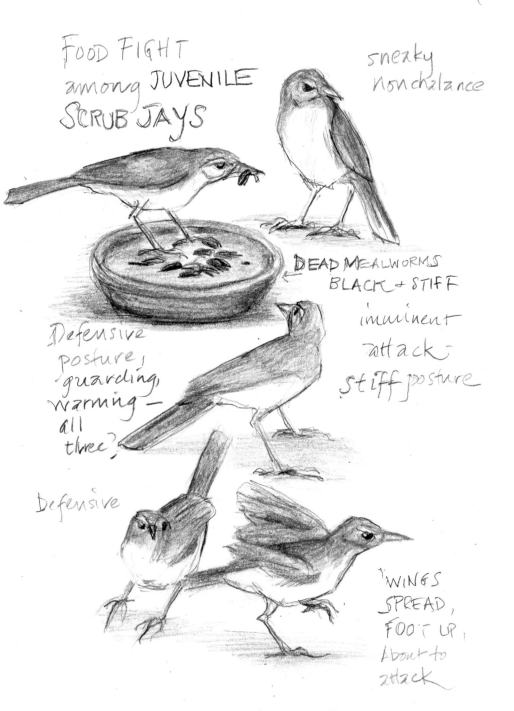

JUNE 30, 2019

FOOD FIGHT
among JUVENILE
SCRUB JAYS

sneaky
nonchalance

← DEAD MEALWORMS
BLACK & STIFF

imminent
attack —
stiff posture

Defensive
posture,
guarding,
warning —
all
three?

Defensive

'WINGS
SPREAD,
FOOT UP,
About to
attack

onto the tail and gave it a jerk. The victim squawked and chased off the aggressor.

A different competitor landed nearby, a Mourning Dove, which instantly puffed up like a hissing cat so that its tiny head was engulfed in mounds of feathers. It no longer looked like an ambassador of peace or marital love. It looked like the Hulk badly disguised as a Mourning Dove. It gave the evil eye to whichever Scrub Jays approached. Like thugs, the Scrubs kept inching forward, their metaphorical switchblades tucked under their wings. Suddenly, the Mourning Dove charged one of the Scrub Jays and launched into mid-flight with sizable talons aimed at its opponent. When the feathers settled, the Mourning Dove proved the winner of the dead mealworms. The losers watched the dove decimate the prize.

The mealworms are dying in this heat faster than the birds can eat them. Today I put another batch of the smelly dead ones in the pan. The young jays gathered. But then a different jay landed next to the pan with a commanding screech. It was an adult. All the young jays scattered into bushes. Slowly they returned and stood nearby, watching their beloved dead mealworms being consumed by the adult, one who likely was their doting parent not that long ago. The adult threatened any that tried to approach. One young bird stood two feet away and cried with its mouth open, fledgling style. *Mama! Feed me!* The adult ignored the beggar. To survive, young birds must learn to fend for themselves.

When the adult left, an enterprising fledgling flew up to an oak tree branch above the empty pan. I could hear it making a knocking sound, not as fast as a woodpecker's drumming, but steady in rhythm. An acorn hit the ground near the pan, startling another jay, and another acorn landed near the bushes. One acorn landed dead center in the pan. After a few more acorns had dropped, the clever fledgling flew down and walked about, proudly inspecting its work. I am not sure whether the young bird was simply an inexperienced bird that dropped the acorns it was supposed to cache, or whether it had intended to drop acorns onto the pan to scare its competitor siblings. If this behavior was indeed deliberate, it's proof I have zero chance of ever outsmarting this bird. Here you go, Scrubster, live mealworms, on the house.

FLEDGLING
SCRUB JAY
MISSING
TAIL

August 3, 2019

I thought I saw a new bird in the yard. It was squatting and appeared unable to move. It had a streaky head, as well as striations over its breast and belly. Through binoculars, I saw it had pink baby lips. Clearly, this was a fledgling. But what species? I could feel my hand drawing it, the angle of the head, like a thumb, the conical beak. I had drawn this bird many times, but what was it? And then an adult Dark-eyed Junco landed two feet away, a male to judge by its long black hood. The females are lighter colored. The mystery bird is his baby, fresh out of the nest. What a transformation it will undergo before it looks like its parent. But already the shapes of a junco are there, just as I had drawn it hundreds of times.

The adult is pecking at seeds on the patio. The fledgling watches and then makes a tentative peck, but in an area without seeds. It moves forward, and this time, it picks up a seed. The adult flies off, apparently satisfied that its fledgling now knows what to do. But wait, the fledgling doesn't know. It is simply sitting on the patio, perfectly still, the seed held in its beak. It tips back its head, as it did in the nest, but it does not know it has to open its beak to release the seed into its mouth. Apparently, that action is not automatic. It is a skill that must be learned, and hopefully before starvation. The baby keeps waving the food in its beak. I am worried. I try to think how I can help this baby learn what to do. Don't interfere with Mother Nature, people would say. And I don't. The fledgling's father has come back with a mealworm.

8·3·19

BABY BIRDS

while learning
how to forage,
it still beseeches
adults
for food

color of baby
junco is more
taupe, like that of
a pine siskin

STREAKY
BREAST —
SEEN IN OTHER
JUVENILE
SPECIES

So fat it
seems impossible
they could ever
fly!

October 13, 2019

My view of seasons no longer follows the Earth's spin axis. Spring, Summer, Fall, and Winter have been replaced by Spring Migration, Nesting Season, Fledging Season, and Fall Migration. The timelines pertain only to birds in my backyard. When I left in mid-September for a month, I knew I might be missing the start of fall migration.

When I finally returned nearly a month later and stepped out onto the patio, I heard a three-note plaintive song. Almost immediately, I saw a beautiful Golden-crowned Sparrow land on the fence, and then another and another and another. Fall migration had indeed arrived. I expect that the White-crowned Sparrow and White-throated Sparrow may come next. Houseguests! Time to spruce up the feeders and prepare extra food.

The Golden-crowned Sparrows are in the front and back yards, on the porch, the verandah, and my bathroom windowsill. I see four or five at a time in each location. They are perched on leafy boughs in the oak trees, scratching the dirt under bushes, bouncing on the branches of the camellia bush by my bathroom window. They are on the fence, the rock wall, the patio furniture, the birdbath stand. They are perched on the top of the umbrella, the top of the feeder station and barbecue grill. I am guessing I have collectively in all locations at least twenty to twenty-five. There are more hummingbirds as well, competitors for feeders, and despite the plentitude, there's no end to the fighting and buzz chases. Competition is a necessary part of life among birds, even when food is plentiful. Who knows when the human might become a slacker and leave for another month. All food must be defended.

Question: Did the same individuals who came last year return to my yard? Why did one Golden-crowned Sparrow repeatedly go to my

OCT 13, 2019

ALASKA

They're back!
GOLDEN CROWNED SPARROW to winter in my yard!

I returned home and immediately saw one on the fence. They remain still for a long time unlike the flitty oak titmouse and chickadee. The Blue Angels roared by and this one was unperturbed. I've been gone a month so I don't know when they came

PLAINTIVE THREE NOTE SONG

I forgot they will also eat from feeder. But mostly they are around feeders. Will see if they like worms.

I hear them singing in the bamboo hedge. Sounds like + looks like I have at least five

Were these birds here last year? They seem familiar with the feeding areas.

bathroom window ledge? Is it because it knows I put seed on this same ledge each morning? It looks at me every now and then, right in the eye. It knows my presence has something to do with food, and not just danger. Otherwise, why does it come when I flip on the bathroom light switch. Okay, time to sprinkle the seeds again. Thanks for reminding me, Golden. Your memory is clearly better than mine, driven by your need to survive and not my pleasure.

AMY TAN

Golden-crowned Sparrow

October 20, 2019

I am glutted with avian delights. More fall migrants are returning. The Lesser Goldfinches are the most conspicuous. They come in gangs. They are almost as tiny as the Anna's Hummingbirds. They eat together, voraciously, dropping three or four intact seeds before eating one. There are six feeder ports, and when twelve jam up the feeders, beak-to-beak battles erupt, and sometimes they fight with their upraised feet. The squabbles also happen when there are only a few birds, and one is apparently occupying a feeder port the other wants. There may be other available ports, but no, that is the one they must have and they must have it now.

When the goldfinches are done eating and making their mess, they leave en masse. Second shift takes over. The ground feeders love the mess dropped by the Lesser Goldfinches. The Fox Sparrows and Hermit Thrushes also come to inspect the offerings. They are ground feeders that usually poke and kick around in the dirt. They often arrive shortly after the migrants return to my yard. They come to eat not just the mess but also the berries and seeds in the trees and bushes.

Unlike the flocks of goldfinches and Golden-crowned Sparrows, the Hermit Thrushes and Fox Sparrows seem to come often alone, and sometimes in pairs. I rarely see more than one at a time. For that reason, they are always exciting to see, even if they do come throughout the day. I use binoculars but am familiar enough with their basic shapes and postures to recognize them from a distance with the naked eye. The Hermit Thrush stands tall on delicately thin legs; its wings are held loose and the bullet-shaped beak is tipped at an upward angle, giving it an aura of privilege and superiority. Its body is a lovely taupe that does not exist in my pencil box, and its rump and tail are rufous, and I have many pencil shades for that. Its front is marked by dark dots and dashes, like secret Morse code. It has big, slightly slanted eyes sur-

OCT 20, 2019
FALL MIGRATION

THEY'RE
BACK!

**LESSER
GOLDFINCH**
- come in groups
- leave as a group
- voracious
- messy eaters,
- juncos eat
  mess

HERMIT THRUSH
I so rarely see him. But
he came to the bathroom
window
ledge
for
seed

I recognized
him by his curved
bill, pretty
round eye and
soft thupe coat

A
beauty!

FOX SPARROW
visits the window sill for
seed. Very streaky and with
part yellow underbill.

rounded by two white crescents. They make the Hermit Thrush look sweet and slightly daft. From my chair at the dining room table, I recognize the chocolate brown Fox Sparrow by its low posture as it hops across the patio, and the periodic wing flutters. It does this a lot, and each flutter lasts only about a second, but it makes the Fox Sparrow look agitated, feisty, easily provoked into a fight, which it often does when there's food around. From drawing birds hundreds, if not thousands of times, I know that the head of a bird has many angles, ones that jut up from the bill, over the eyes, flat across the crown and back down the slope to the neck and shoulders. The Fox Sparrow, however, looks like it has a very round head. I wind up drawing cartoon birds because I am drawing what I think it looks like, and not what I see. Its head is not perfectly round. Like that of the Hermit Thrush, the main color of the Fox Sparrow is one that I lack in my pencil box. I have to blend—a chocolate brown with a bit of red or burgundy or purple, or something else, I don't know what. But some Fox Sparrows are slate brown. So I blend a deep brown and warm gray, or I start with a base of gray and add warm brown. I try many browns and grays. I know that feathers are never one color. They contain reflections of colors. I can never get the color to be as beautiful and as deeply saturated as the bird's plumage truly is. The front of the Fox Sparrow is white and marked with a dark chevron pattern. The bill is marked with a dab of yellow on the lower mandible.

I have learned to look for these field marks by drawing them over and over again. I am secretly proud when I make the correct ID of a bird in front of others. I hope I don't ever come across as a smart ass. I have a long way to go before I am qualified to be one. I am still in a newbie stage, often wrong, often surprised, often puzzled. I know too little to know what's ordinary. But I have heard experienced birders call the Lesser Goldfinch a "trash bird" because it is so common and numerous. I heard others call a House Sparrow a "junk" bird, an invasive, like the European Starling. I understand the antipathy. Invasive birds usurp habitat and resources. But I can't help but feel discomfort. The rhetoric is often the same as the racist ones I hear about Chinese people.

I am still new to birding, and so every bird is a good bird to see, even the ones I see all the time. I am happy they've come, that they've chosen my yard to visit for a few minutes or the day or every day for many weeks or months. I especially love the birds that are here every day of the year, like the titmouse and chickadee. I hope I never cease to be amazed.

GOLDEN-CROWNED
SPARROW LOOKING
AT ITS FEET

October 21, 2019

A sickening thud. Heartbreak. A Hermit Thrush hit the window where two anti-collision decals had fallen off. This is one of six fatalities I have seen in six and a half years of living in this house. Each one has left me gutted and more determined to find a way to stop the window strikes. It is a challenge because the house is nearly all glass on three sides of our main floor, the open space that comprises our living room and dining room. Even before I became wild about wild birds, I wanted to build a house that looked like an aerie, a pavilion floating in trees. We succeeded in building that, too successfully. Sometimes, a new bird to the yard mistakenly thinks it can fly through. Fortunately, the window collisions happen only on one side. Unfortunately, it is the side I watch each day, the patio off the dining area.

As prevention, I have tried Halloween decals of spider webs, which are black and ugly. But birds still hit the windows, although not nearly as hard. A bonk instead of a thud. Most flew away without stopping. I got UV decals in a pattern of leaves. I still heard bonks on occasion. Then I got many more UV decals. I got a Halloween mask in hopes birds would avoid a face. Some might say one collision death a year is not many. I read a post by someone who has several window collision deaths a day. To me, the death of even one bird is one too many. It's tragic and I feel sickened with guilt.

I told Bernd Heinrich about the recent fatality, and he said that ovenbirds, a migrant warbler, sometimes hit a particular window of his cabin in the deep Maine woods. He said they fly low and accelerate fast and their head-on collisions tend to be fatal. He uses any dead animal he finds as an opportunity to study the behavior of scavengers, be they ravens or maggots. So I try to use the opportunity to learn as well. I picked up the Hermit Thrush. It was still warm and floppy. I

~ HERMIT THRUSH ~

WINDOW STRIKE FATALITY
OCCURED WHERE TWO UV
DECALS HAD FALLEN OFF,
ACCORDING TO JACK DUMBACHER
AT CALACADEMY. THRUSHES. OFTEN VICTIMS

RIP
HERMIT
THRUSH
BELOVED
OCT 21, 2019

OF SIX FATALITIES
IN SIX AND A HALF YEARS, THREE
WERE HERMIT THRUSHES. THEIR
ACCELERATION MUST
BE FASTER
THAN
MOST,

NOTE: DORSAL MIDLINE
DISTRIBUTION OF FEATHERS

CONSOLATION
THIS BIRD
WILL GO TO
CALACADEMY
TO BE PRESERVED
AND STUDIED

HEAD FEATHER
PATTERN HAS
MULTI-DIRECTIONAL
PATTERNS AND "SPOTS" FALL
INTO LINE & NOT COMPLETELY
RANDOM,

studied the intricate feathers on its head, how they lie in a multidirectional pattern according to different parts of the head. The spots I see on its breast from a distance follow a pattern as well and are not randomly placed. These fine details made me appreciate this bird even more, and I also felt sadder. I drew it as it looked, its eyes closed, feet already stiffened, the feathers of one wing splayed. A beautiful bird, even in death.

I could not bear to throw it in the trash. I debated leaving it out in the open as food for a predator. Happily, Jack Dumbacher, curator of the Bird and Mammal Department of the California Academy of Sciences, said he would be glad to take it next week. I carefully wrapped the thrush in a paper towel and placed it in a plastic food container. Three thousand live mealworms in the fridge, and now a dead Hermit Thrush in the freezer. I have a very understanding husband. The thrush will rest in the freezer until Jack Dumbacher can retrieve it. At Cal Academy, a recent graduate from Cornell will skin the bird, stuff it with tissue, and label it with the date and location where it was found. The Hermit Thrush will become part of their scientific collection for time immemorial. It will have a higher purpose it never intended, and that is consolation to me.

October 29, 2019

Hermit Thrushes rarely visit backyards and generally do not
visit feeders.

—*Cornell Lab of Ornithology*

Today, a Hermit Thrush that often comes to my backyard spent
about two and a half hours trying to break into three feeders.
Defying stereotype, it was hardly shy but stared right at me as I took
photos. It watched other birds entering the cage feeders and tried to
go in after them but could not figure out how to fit between the spaces
of the grid. It was probably a bit too long and leggy to fit cleanly,
although Golden-crowned Sparrows, which are about the same size
in length and bigger in girth, easily go in and out. I think the Hermit
Thrush's difficulty has to do with its usual posture. It stands nearly
upright, like Scrub Jays, and this one did not know how to crouch to
fit into a tiny space.

I was entertained watching it attempt various strategies. It sat on
top of one feeder and peered down into the cage. It circled the top
looking in from all angles. It then jumped onto a hummingbird swing
with a little red glass bead. At first, it lost its balance on the swing but
after three or four falls, it learned how to balance and perch. Another
cage feeder was next to the swing, and the thrush stretched its neck
toward the seeds on the other side of the bars. Then it took an interest
in the red glass bead above its head. Perhaps it thought the bead was a
berry, which Hermit Thrushes like to eat. It tried landing on an open
Squirrel Buster feeder that required it to balance on a little perch. It
did not understand the concept of perching and instead landed on the
feeder sideways and fell off.

I placed live mealworms in the dirt of the flowerpot right below the
feeders. The other ground feeders went wild for them—the Golden-

crowned Sparrows, California Towhee, Spotted Towhee, and Dark-eyed Junco. But the Hermit Thrush remained interested in only the feeders above. So focused. So determined.

How does a ground feeder learn to become a perching feeder bird? Why was this thrush so persistent in doing what it normally does not do and also cannot easily do? Why would it choose the harder way to obtain food when the same offerings—sunflower seeds and live mealworms—were available out in the open? Was it a young, inexperienced bird? Was it migrating and curious about these unfamiliar but promising food sources? How much does curiosity and persistence play a role in a bird's chances of survival?

I have a new opinion of Hermit Thrushes. They are not shy and secretive. They are solitary nonconformists.

November 9, 2019

Now that the migrants are returning in greater numbers, I have added more feeders to each of the four locations: the patio, the verandah, the office porch, and on the other side of the bathroom window. Sichuan Sunflower Seeds. Vindaloo Suet Mini Balls. Farm-raised Mealworms. Vegan Nectar. Spicy Suet. Nuts & Chews & Bugs. Nyjer Nirvana. Graines Pour Oiseaux Sauvages. Alaskan Taste Water. These are signs of my descent into madness.

The worm bowl must be refilled daily and the seed feeders every few days. I now order 5,000 live mealworms each week and spend an hour or more wangling them into containers, while wearing gloves and also a mask to avoid breathing floating bits of cast-off exoskeletons. Although I've done this chore numerous times, the sensation of them writhing in my hands is still creepy. They are trying to escape, I sense that. They know what awaits.

Hummingbird feeders must be disinfected every few days (more often in hot weather) and refilled with fresh nectar. It takes an hour to clean seven of them. The hummingbirds are disturbed by the missing feeders. They are obsessive in returning to the same spots where the feeders once hung.

My favorite feeding ritual is to toss seeds onto the sill of my bathroom window. All the ground feeders visit the sill and dramas unfold. The birds arrive from within the camellia bush, like characters stepping out from behind the opera stage curtain. A posse of quail. A junco pair. A bird I have never seen before. Today a White-crowned Sparrow came to the sill, the first one I have seen this year. It has both the whitest stripes and the yellowest beak of any bird in the yard. For that bird alone, all that time and expense of feeding my feathery visitors have been worth it.

Nov 9, 2019

DUSK SPECIALS

SPICY SUET

JUST LIKE THE STUFF MOM USED TO THROW UP FOR YOU. INCLUDES SEEDS, INSECTS, AND NASTY MEALWORMS.

☆ MIGRATORY STAR AWARD ☆

NUTS & CHEWS & BUGS

WINNER OF THE 2018 SCRUB JAY AWARD for BEST LOOT

BUGS, FAT. SEED. GRAINES AND LOTS OF CAYENNE SEASONING.

NYJER NIRVANA

IF YOU'RE A BUSY FINCH AND HAVE NO TIME TO CATCH, ORDER SOME OF OUR G.M.O. THISTLE. A CROWD PLEASER.

GREAT FOR PIGEON PARTIES

GRAINES POUR OISEAUX SAUVAGES

IF YOU'RE FEELING SAUVAGE COME HAVE A BEAKFUL OF MILLET.

GOOD FOR BATHING and DRINKING

"ALASKAN TASTE" WATER "DUNK 'n DRUNK."

WHY GO ALL WAY NORTH FOR MELTED ICE CAP? WE HAVE FLOODS OF WATER!

November 11, 2019

Several people have asked if I recognize individual birds in the yard. I don't, not with any confidence, unless the bird is missing a leg, or has lost its tail, or is the only one of its kind. Their question, though, made me wonder why I have never attempted to recognize individuals so I can greet them by name. *Hey there, Betty Bewick's Wren!* I have never thought to name them. Even though I feed them as some might domesticated birds, meaning on a regular basis, I appreciate that they are wild. They do not belong to me.

But now that so many birds are coming, I would like to know more accurately how many of each species are here from day to day. If I see three Oak Titmice on the back porch, how do I know the three on the patio are not the same ones in the back? I can differentiate some birds by sex, if the males and females have different plumage. And some may be distinctive by their behavior. When I put seeds out on the windowsill, the first bird to come is either a dark male junco or a non-breeding Golden-crowned Sparrow. Actually, sometimes they come as soon as they see my face. I should pay more attention to see if these are the same birds each morning. Within seconds, however, other birds come to the windowsill and I am done in by sensory overload. I can't use a bird's size as a reliable way to differentiate them. Birds are shapeshifters. The large one could be the same as the slender one. With chickadees, it's difficult to tell them apart because they flit in quickly and leave quickly, and there are many of them. But the Dark-eyed Juncos come frequently and remain at the feeder or on the bathroom sill for 45–60 seconds or more, giving me enough time to make observations. I decided to use the juncos as a way to create a method for individual identification. I might use this to at least sort out which are males and which are females. The system I devised is based on coloration. The juncos are ideal for that. They have a

Nov 11, 2019

HOW MANY ARE IN THE JUNCO CLAN?

Determining by color variation

HEAD COLOR EXTENDS TO BREAST

STOPS AT THROAT

simple body structure, and the different colors are particular to areas of the body. I sketched templates of juncos of slightly different sizes, just their outlines. I then made a palette of colors, rows with different shades of pink, peach, brown, gray, black, and so forth. I identified six areas to check for color: the head, breast, wing, mantle, tail, and flank. I decided I should also note the length of the hood, whether it stops at the throat or extends to the breast, since that is a good way to differentiate females from males. With this system, I would be able to quickly fill in a bird template with on-the-spot color observations.

My system is proving to be rather disorganized and impractical. I can't color in fast enough. I forget to note the length of the hood, the color of the undersides. Thank God I am not a scientist. Maybe I can simply shorthand it to Sibley's description of dark male adult, pale male adult, sooty female adult, plus a few variations for juveniles and first winter birds. But right now, it seems like all the Dark-eyed Juncos are males with long black hoods. I thought about focusing more on seeing an overall pattern with each bird—a gestalt. But birds don't see each other as gestalts, any more than I see another Asian person as looking just like me. It is important to know the specific size and color since they may relate to dominance over food, territory, and females. Do darker-colored individuals displace females and younger males? If two males are competing, is there anything about their coloration that other males recognize as belonging to the more dominant male? Or is dominance signaled by foot size, or more feathers on the chest, and other things I cannot distinguish? What do birds see?

I am sensing more the importance of knowing the specific colors of each bird. Some juncos I have seen will eat cooperatively in the same place, just six to eight inches apart. Is their coloration similar? Are there both males and females in the group? Are younger males lighter in color? I feel like I am sorting out my sock drawer and finding singletons instead of pairs.

I also decided to follow up on a theory I have about dominance among Golden-crowned Sparrows. The female and male supposedly have the same plumage, but the males may be slightly bigger. That doesn't help me. I see Golden-crowned Sparrows in many sizes. As I noted a while ago, the shapeshifter factor may be in play, but I also sense there is more variation in size than simply one related to sex. The ones with the most intensely colored heads—with the thickest black lateral crown stripes (brows) and brightest yellow crowns—tend to be the more dominant. Then again, those are breeding plumage colors, and those birds are older than the birds with brown brows and only a smidge of yellow on their crown. It makes sense to me that dominance and plumage change with age. But would two birds of the same age have noticeably different black brows and yellow crowns?

Also, how should I assess what counts as dominant behavior? A bird may chase another from the windowsill. But my presence may be a factor in which birds remain on the sill. Some birds are familiar with me. They are less apt to flee if they see me in the window. A lower-ranking bird could conceivably remain on the sill chowing down on seeds, while its much more dominant counterpart is fuming in nearby branches, waiting for me to leave so it can assert itself.

Will I ever know enough to be able to distinguish individuals one from the other? Is my inability to recognize birds similar to white people thinking all Asians look alike? Do birds recognize individual birds of their own kind in the same vicinity? What details do they see that we humans don't? Do they recognize their adult progeny or nest-mates? Do they recognize one-season mates? Do they recognize me? Maybe I should first ask *why* they would need to remember another bird or human?

November 14, 2019

The day began as usual. During the bird feeding happy hour, the camellia bush by the bathroom window was bustling with sparrows, chickadees, goldfinches, and the ever-present Golden-crowned Sparrows. I was standing near the bathroom window when I spotted what I thought was an immature White-crowned Sparrow with its distinctive yellow bill. I knew this bird well since I had drawn a detailed portrait of it the year before and had studied its coloration, which is different from an adult's. I first saw this same bird a few hours earlier, eating mess on the back porch among five or six Golden-crowned Sparrows. It was now sitting on the branch next to a shepherd's hook, about a foot and a half away from the window. Instead of the black brows and white crown of the adult White-crowned Sparrow, this young bird had rufous brows and a taupe crown and face. I like drawing the immature version of this bird because I think it is prettier than the more boldly colored adult.

I looked more closely at the bird near the window. Its face was actually more gray than taupe. So was this a song sparrow? I instantly ruled that out. The face of this bird was not demarcated by areas of gray, white, and rufous like that of a song sparrow. Also, a song sparrow would have a gray bill, not yellow, and its breast would be heavily streaked, not clear. The mystery bird turned toward me, and then I saw the signature black spot on the clear breast. I went giddy in the brain. It was an *American Tree Sparrow*. But how could that be? This was not a bird you'd see on the West Coast, let alone in my backyard. I stared at it for ten seconds, reciting aloud the differentiating field marks in my head to encode them into memory, and then rushed to get my camera in the next room. No one would believe what I saw unless I had a photo. When I returned, the bird was gone. I quickly

MYSTERY
BIRD
11/14/19

WHITE-CROWNED SPARROW IMMATURE?

The bushes by the bathroom window Were full of sparrows!

I saw one with a yellow bill and then a rufous crown. Aha! An immature white-crowned sparrow. I had seen many

SONG SPARROW?

BICOLOR BILL

VAGRANT JACKPOT!

AMERICAN TREE SPARROW

But then the cheeks (malar) had a more grey blue, like that of a Song Sparrow. But the bill was grey and it had a more defined pattern. I couldn't see if the mystery birds breast was streaked

And then it turned toward me and I saw the breast spot. AMERICAN TREE SPARROW — a rare vagrant!

sketched the process of elimination I had applied to identify a bird I never should have seen.

There was a reason I knew so clearly what this bird looked like. Last year, when I was in New York, I drew an American Tree Sparrow in detail in hopes that I would recognize it in Central Park. I studied many photos while drawing it. I followed reports of its migratory path. But I never saw the bird, because by the end of my stay it had not migrated any farther south than Boston. After seeing the bird by my window, I pulled out the detailed drawing I made the year before. What I had perceived as a yellow bill was actually a bicolor bill—a gray upper mandible and yellow lower mandible. But everything else I noted was right on the mark. It's a common enough bird on the East Coast, but if this bird was what I thought it was, it would be a rare vagrant in California. I went to my eBird app to see if anyone had reported one. Nope. I debated for a while whether to report it, knowing that if I did, it would be flagged by a monitor. And it was, immediately. I had no photo, I told him, and expected my report to be discounted. But he found my sketches showing the field marks of each of the bird species I had considered in those few seconds to be even better than a photo. Happily, I also learned from the monitor, he had spotted an American Tree Sparrow in Point Reyes but had not yet reported it. It was within a mixed group of Golden-crowned Sparrows, which lent credence to my claim that one had made its way to our yard and was with a group of Golden-crowned Sparrows. Hardcore birders flocked to Point Reyes to find the star vagrant. But it was not seen again. Could the bird in my yard possibly have been the same bird? The monitor thought that it was possible. It was rare to have one. It would be rarer to have more than one. Only two years ago, I would not have noticed that bird at all. How many other yards had this same bird visited, places where people paid no attention to little brown birds?

Now the questions: Why did this vagrant wind up in northern California? Why would it be in my yard, one that has trees and bushes, and not the habitat it prefers, the open space and shrubs found in places like Point Reyes? Ironically, despite its name, it is not a bird typically found in trees. Was it a young bird who joined up with the wrong gang of sparrows, and when they migrated south, it went with them? Will it continue to hang with them? Will the other sparrows allow it to remain? Do sparrows recognize they are not with their own kind? Are they submissive if they are party crashers? Will this sparrow remain in northern California and continue to be seen elsewhere? If not, why would it leave? If it does stay, when it's time to migrate back north to its summer home, will it follow the Golden-crowned Sparrows to their northern home in Alaska or northern Canada? Is that an area where other American Tree Sparrows also live? Or will it try to find its own home elsewhere to be with its own kind? Will it become disoriented and die? Will I ever know the answer to even one of these questions?

For now, I can only imagine what might happen. I am highly skilled at doing that. Stories about lost souls abound in fiction.

November 22, 2019

I saw a Fox Sparrow on the windowsill, sitting motionless for at least five minutes, despite my presence. These sparrows have never been easily scared off. But to remain this long was unusual. I came closer to the window and looked down. Its right foot was a tangled mess. It appeared to have chewing gum on its toes such that half its foot was welded into a tight fist. The left foot was also affected, although not quite as badly. Had it landed on a sticky substance like tree sap or gum? Or maybe it had flown down from the fires up north after it had seared its feet landing on a hot branch or dirt covered in embers. Those were the possibilities I conjured up to avoid thinking of something worse: avian pox, a contagious disease.

The Fox Sparrow looked down at its feet, as if wondering what was hindering its movement. Its body was puffed up, and combined with its stillness, I knew that the bird was clearly in distress. Was it in pain? One good sign: It was eating heartily. It jumped down onto the ground and was a bit clumsy when standing or walking. Its rump was dirty, which made me think it might be dragging itself. Since it was a ground feeder, and not a perching bird, this was a bad condition for it to be in. It travels through leaf litter and uses its feet to dig for insects. It finds shelter in ground coverings, and nests on the ground or among the upraised roots at the foot of a tree. But what if the ground is wet and it must perch to stay dry? Can it sleep for long periods on a branch? With deformed feet that cannot bend, it could not possibly perch for any amount of time. As if to contradict me, it flew up and perched on a nearby branch in the camellia bush. A minute later, it returned to the windowsill. It continued to go back and forth between the bush and windowsill at least three times—three being the number of times I happened to see it when I went by throughout the day. For all I knew, it could have been flying back and forth dozens of times throughout the day.

Nov 22, 2019

The Sad Story of the Fat Bird

Whenever I see
a puffed up
bird, I know
I am seeing
a bird who
may be
sick or
injured

FOX
SPARROW

GUM
OR
? AVIAN POX

DISTORTED
FOOT /
FEET

He came and sat on
the sill eating
seeds, unable
to walk.
He
shuffled
and
hopped

At one point
he looked
down at
his foot, was
it painful?
Was he wondering
what was on
his foot?

GROWTH
ON
BOTH
FEET

Dirt
on back
end.

He can still fly
and even perch.

But in thinking he drags himself on
his bottom or belly. He has dirt
clinging at the back. He depends on easy
food and goes to the sill often.

If it was avian pox, I should stop putting seeds out to discourage this bird and others from coming. There are at least two other Fox Sparrows in the yard, and many kinds of birds also come to the windowsill for seeds. Although birds don't necessarily die from the pox, it is contagious. The disease supposedly clears up after a few weeks. If it is on the face, however, and impedes seeing or eating, a bird would likely die of starvation or be easy pickings for a hawk. But if this is indeed an injury, like a burn sustained from the fires up north, and if I do not put seeds out, it will be deprived of a food source it truly depends on.

I tried to capture the Fox Sparrow so I could take it to a wildlife rehab center. But it still flew well enough to avoid me. I made the hard, hard decision to stop putting out seed. I sprayed 2% hydrogen peroxide to disinfect the windowsill of contagion. If the Fox Sparrow landed on the damp sill, the disinfectant might help.

It is remarkable what birds can endure. It is tragic what they cannot. I am hoping this bird is remarkable.

AMY TAN
FOX SPARROW
2023

Fox Sparrow

Thanksgiving Day, November 28, 2019

At 11:30 a.m. there was an inundation of songbirds at the feeder, as if they were Black Friday shoppers frantic to snap up good deals on worms. At 3:30 p.m., the same happened. The patio was swarming with about fifteen or more Golden-crowned Sparrows, and in smaller numbers, Chestnut-backed Chickadees, Pygmy Nuthatches, Dark-eyed Juncos, a Hermit Thrush, a Fox Sparrow, a White-crowned Sparrow, four Townsend's Warblers, several Lesser Goldfinches, two Oak Titmice, a Downy Woodpecker, several Anna's Hummingbirds—three males and one female—and a rarely seen Brown Creeper. Birds were streaking across the patio, darting into shrubs and popping out of them, running across the elevated planters. Birds on adrenaline. About ten flew out of shrubs when Bobo came running up the stairs barking his head off to announce "I'm here, everyone!" The birds returned. As always, they have no lasting fear of this landbound four-pound dog. But it's awfully nice of them to scatter and give him a thrill.

I am thankful to the birds that regularly visit my yard. I am thankful for the abundance of them today. I have put out extra helpings of mealworms, more suet, a feast of gratitude on this Thanksgiving Day.

THANKSGIVING GUESTS
THANKS TO THE BIRDS
WHO CAME TO MY BACKYARD IN 2019

DOWNY
WOODPECKER

WOODPECKERS AND
BROWN CREEPER
REMIND ME OF ROACHES
AS THEY SCURRY ACROSS
TREE TRUNKS. THIS
DOWNY WAS ON A
MASSIVE LIMB THAT
GIVE CLUE TO HOW
SMALL IT IS, 6"-8".
IT ATE IN BARE SPOTS
BETWEEN LICHEN.
WHAT ARE THE RED TREE
VEINS? CAPILLARY
SYSTEM? DISEASE?

WHEN ONE DARK-EYED JUNCO
COMES, THREE SOON FOLLOW

December 4, 2019

When I first took an interest in birds, I asked on a Facebook bird group page what kind of food I should put in a feeder for sparrows. The curt answer from one expert was this: All sparrows are ground feeders and do not eat from feeders. He suggested I get a guidebook on birds so I could learn the basics (meaning, don't ask questions that are common knowledge). I was new to watching birds, so I felt like an idiot. I often do when some pooh-bah issues a blunt answer in subjects I know little about. Fortunately, most people who love birds are kind toward beginner birders. In fact, every birder and nature journaler I've personally met is exceedingly kind and patient with every beginner. They love to instill a love of birds.

The pooh-bah was right. Sparrows are ground feeders. They peck at food on the ground. They dig into dirt. But one day, it occurred to me that ground feeders might be taught to use cage feeders through graduated learning. I created square feeders out of 12" x 12" grid panels and placed them on the ground. The sparrows could easily access them, once they overcame their trepidation of entering an enclosed space. Build a cage feeder, they will come, especially if the lure is live mealworms. Over time, I suspended the cages and added a plastic bottom so the sparrows could stand as they do on ground. They took to entering those feeders almost immediately. Then I took away the flat bottom panel. They continued to enter the cages and learned to perch on the grid wire and edges of the bowl. They eventually ate at store-bought feeders with perches. The new behavior was learned. They were motivated to adapt. There was no inability that was innate, no physiological impediment to their being able to perch to eat. All the ground feeders learned to do this—the many kinds of sparrows, including the tubby California Towhees, and even the secretive Fox Sparrow. He bullies all the other sparrows in the cage.

GROUND FEEDERS IN MY YARD ALSO PERCH BUT PERCHERS DON'T GROUND FEED. HOW EASY IS IT TO LEARN EITHER?

DARK-EYED JUNCO IS A GROUND FEEDER BUT PERCHES ON MY FEEDERS. NO "FANCY" PERCHING

HOOKED 1ST TOE TO BAR

— WHAT IS OTHER TOE DOING?
TOE
— HANGS LOOSELY

GRASPS 2ND BAR

I'M MOTIVATED BY WORMS!

I'LL TRY ANYTHING TO GET FOOD BUT THE PERCHES ARE TOO SMALL

BAND-TAILED PIGEON

OAK TITMOUSE USES ALL FOUR TOES TO GRASP ONTO BARS AND THIN BRANCHES. HE IS A BORN PERCHER AND APPEARS TO ME TO BE SHOWING OFF ACROBATIC UPSIDE DOWN OR EVEN SIDEWAYS PERCHING, HE LANDS ON SLIPPERY BARS, BUT ALSO FEEDS ON THE SILL

OTHER SMALL BIRDS HAVE VERSATILE PERCHING SKILLS, e.g. NUTHATCHES THAT HANG UPSIDE DOWN OR SIDEWAYS, AND CHICKADEES THAT GO BACK & FORTH FROM TREE TO PERCH OFTEN

But what about the reverse? Birds that perched at feeders, I noticed, never ate on the ground. That was true of the finches, titmice, chickadees, and nuthatches. Why? Both the ground feeders and the feeder birds are in the same taxonomical order of Passerines, distinguished by their foot structure, three toes forward and one toe back. (I've drawn those feet thousands of times, and it is still difficult for me to capture how they wrap around branches and poles. It is so much easier to draw a foot when the bird is standing on terra firma.) If the little songbirds are endowed with similar feet, what else is at play that prevents a feeder bird from eating the same food that I put on the ground? All they have to do is jump down, right? A chickadee and titmouse could peck at a seed it holds on flat ground, just as easily as it does on a branch higher up. No? Could I set up a graduated learning process by, say, placing food on platform feeders closer and closer to the ground, until the platform is right on the ground? If I then removed the platform entirely, would they be able to make the final short leap to eating on flat ground? Or would they do this more readily if I removed all feeders except those on the ground?

I once saw an Oak Titmouse clamp on to four or five mealworms to carry back to the nest. But as it prepared to take off, one or two mealworms slipped out of its bill and fell to the ground. The Oak Titmouse looked down to see where the fallen mealworms went, but then—*oh, well la-dee-dah, too bad*—it flew off, not bothering to scoop them up. I have seen Dark-eyed Juncos do something similar—grab an excessive number of mealworms, only to drop one or two. The junco, a ground feeder, would always fly down to pick them up.

Maybe their unwillingness has something to do with their protective instincts. Perhaps birds that perch at feeders have an innate sense of caution around open spaces on the ground. Or perhaps their foot size is smaller and weaker than a ground feeder's and that makes it hard to propel themselves into flight from the ground to escape a predator.

Or maybe it's because they cannot quickly hop. I noticed that ground feeders are adept at running along the top of the fence to gain the best position for landing on a feeder. Actually, it only looks like running. Their locomotion does not involve alternating legs and feet the way that humans and ravens move. The ground feeders move in bursts of hops, so fast and low to the ground they appear to be smoothly running. In contrast, when a titmouse or nuthatch lands on the fence, its next move is to fly to the feeder stand, and then to a particular feeder. Although the sparrows are bigger than titmice and nuthatches, diminutive size alone can't be the reason certain birds don't feed on the ground. The Bewick's Wren is smaller than a titmouse. It perches on feeders, eats from the ground, and hops quickly across the patio.

Why am I obsessing over these questions? Maybe part of it stems from a perverse desire to prove the pooh-bah wrong.

December 9, 2019

When I go looking for birds, it's like the game "Where's Waldo?" I can see birds more readily if they are moving around and a branch bounces. Once I spot a bird in clear view, I might do a rough sketch, and often I take a photo so that I can later draw something more refined, even though it is out of context. In doing nature journaling, however, I feel it is important to include the context. It says a lot about what the bird is doing. And why.

The *why* is essential. That behavior in context enables me to understand the bird. Easier said than done. It's hard to draw the context—the camellia bush, the spaces between leaves where I can see the birds hiding, the different species, the relative size of the leaves to the birds, the weather, the temperature, the time of day, all of which might influence what the bird is doing. How much of the bush should I draw? The 10 a.m. scene is less active than the 3 p.m. surge when birds come out to chow down before sunset. How do I suggest what is going on with only pencil sketches?

I decided to give a sense of what it is like to see many different birds in the camellia bush when I am brushing my teeth looking out my bathroom window. I include no details of the birds or leaves. I created a solid tonal background of graphite. I then used a small mono eraser to remove tone to create silhouettes of leaves and birds in the bush. The spots with birds are slightly different. Those are clues as to where the birds are.

When people compliment bird drawings, mine or others', saying they are "better than Audubon," they don't realize that there is a lot more that Audubon did than simply draw feathers on a bird, apart from being a racist slave owner. He took on the feat of drawing all the birds in America, tracking them down, capturing both their habitat and a signature behavior. The Ivory-billed Woodpeckers are depicted

WHERE'S JUNCO? 12-9-19

WHAT I SAW

Sometimes I get
caught up in creating
the pretty picture, and
I take my subject out
of context. This is what it's really
like looking for birds.

pulling bark from a dead tree to get to crevices of insects. Pairs of Mourning Doves are courting among the white blossoms of a silky camellia bush. My birds are on universal all-purpose branches and among unidentifiable all-purpose leaves. I have a long ways to go. It is not about my getting better at drawing branches or leaves. It is drawing with more knowledge of the bird and its very particular place in the world.

DARK-EYED
JUNCO

December 21, 2019

Live commentary! The Windowsill Wars are heating up. Among the contestants: The Dark-eyed Junco, Lesser Goldfinch, Fox Sparrow, White-throated Sparrow, Townsend's Warbler, Golden-crowned Sparrow—and today's surprise challenger—the Hermit Thrush, who has shed its reclusive nature and is now a regular guest on the backyard patio, as well as on the bathroom windowsill. Today's winner will lay claim to all the sunflower seeds in the pile I made on the sill.

It begins. The Dark-eyed Junco jumps down from the shepherd's hook and nonchalantly eats a seed. A Golden-crowned Sparrow does a surprise jump-stomp side attack, sending the junco flying. Another Golden-crowned hidden in the bush has just landed quietly behind the first Golden-crowned and initiates a measured series of hops toward the first. But a Fox Sparrow's sudden descent chases away both the sneaky Golden-crowned and its intended victim. A second later, the same Golden-crowned returns and lands near the Fox Sparrow, causing it to flee into the camellia bush. The Golden-crowned hops around, back and forth, eating seeds, standing tall with a raised brow (supercilium) and bristled raised crest feathers. When it turns, a Hermit Thrush nearly bumps into it face on, and the Golden-crowned flies off, but returns a second later. The slender Hermit Thrush stands tall on its spindly legs, stretching upward with its bill upraised, which gives it a snooty demeanor. It flicks its wings. Is the wing movement agitation? Or is it a defensive or offensive signal to its competitor? A showdown is about to happen. The Golden-crowned Sparrow goes into a horizontal pose, crouching low, extending its neck, making itself torpedo-like. It does wing-flapping jumps forward. The Hermit Thrush gives a warning cry. Or is that a cry of alarm? It turns its back on the Golden-crowned, an odd move. Is this a bird's version of superiority or submission? By avoiding eye contact, is it placating the sparrow so it might be allowed to stay? It eats a few seeds. Whatever the thrush's intention was with that tail-in-your-face move, it scores no brownie points. The Golden-crowned Sparrow shoves him off the ledge and tastes victory—the pile of seeds on the sill—for only a few seconds. A male California Quail jumps onto the sill and the Golden-crowned moves to the other end, watching. A second later, Mr. Quail's entire clan of wives and kids are plopping down. The Golden-crowned Sparrow is crowded out. A feeding frenzy among twelve quail ensues, their heads and feathery plumes bobbing like speed typists as they peck the sill. Ding! Done! In three minutes, the seeds are decimated.

It's a landslide victory. New Champion of the Windowsill Wars: The Family Quail! After they depart, I will put out more seeds for the losers.

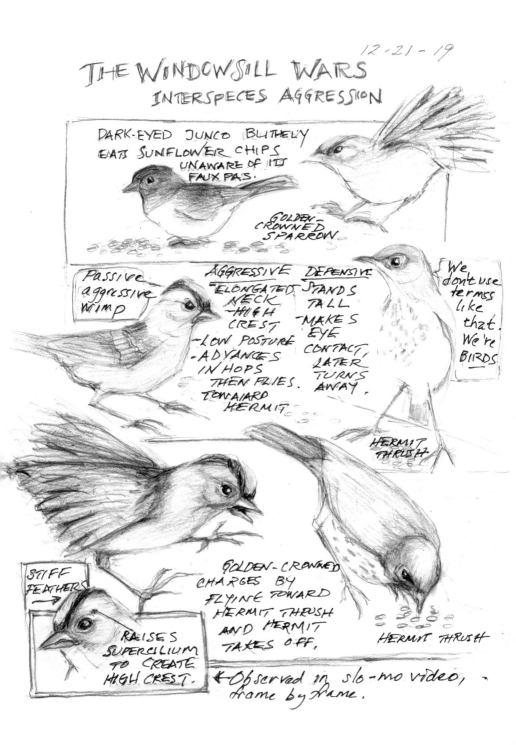

Golden-crowned Sparrow

AMY TAN

Dark-eyed Junco

Lesser Goldfinch

Band-tailed Pigeon

California Towhee

Bewick's Wren (fledgling)

American Crow

CALIFORNIA SCRUB JAY
A. TAN
30 MARCH 2020
(21 DAYS IN ISOLATION)

California Scrub Jay

January 1, 2020

For a year, I would hear a rhythmic typing sound every now and then. I pointed it out to my nature journal mentor, Fiona, one afternoon when she was visiting, and she immediately told me it was a Ruby-crowned Kinglet. To judge by the direction of the sound, she said, it was near the top of the oak trees, a typical place where these birds are found. When I finally saw the tiny yellow bird at the suet feeder, it did not sit still for more than a second before it shot out and returned to the inner bowers of an oak tree. Throughout the day, it flirted with my curiosity, and was gone by the time my jaw dropped.

On December 28, the day of the Christmas Bird Count in Sausalito, I was with Fiona, her mother, Beth, and our leader and friend, Bob Atwood. After birding around Fort Baker, we decided to stop by my house for lunch and, hopefully, to spot a few birds to add to the count. Just past the gate, we saw fluttering movements in the small tree on the left. A Ruby-crowned Kinglet was eating berries, as was a Hermit Thrush. Both birds stood on their toes, their bills tipped straight up to reach the berries that were nearly out of reach. Adrenaline rush. The kinglet was so close I could have touched it. For the first time I could see it well, and for some reason, it did not fly away as I admired those enormous, perfectly round dark eyes. With its white eye ring, it resembled a living cartoon character. Those two birds were added to our Christmas Bird Count.

Since that day, the kinglet has appeared daily at the suet cake feeders. More new birds will come, I can feel it. I cannot command them to come, so when they do visit, I feel hope enough to override the dread I sometimes feel for what may be coming for planet Earth.

January 1, 2020

For a year, I heard it as a typing sound — chk! chk! chk-chk! — no ring. I saw its bouncing movement within trees. On Dec 28, it came out onto the feeder.

CHK!
CHK!
CHK!

RUBY CROWNED KINGLET

YELLOW "BOOTS"

I have never seen the ruby crown.

It loves suet!

It was constant bouncy movement in a tree.

January 7, 2020

My biologist friend Lucia Jacobs told me that her current research concerned "food-rich" squirrels, meaning they have more than they can eat. Each squirrel can hide in different locations more than a thousand pieces of food in a year. They need to later remember where to find them. I don't need to be a scientist to know that squirrels have amazing memories. Once they discover how to break into a feeder, they never forget where to go for a quick snack.

Lucia is interested in doing research on the memory skills of Scrub Jays as well, which vie with those of squirrels. I had already read that California Scrub Jays store a lot of acorns, one source saying it was 3,500 to 6,000 acorns a year. Unfathomable. What researcher counted those? Why would a Scrub Jay need to hide thousands of acorns? And why are they spending so much time breaking into my feeders instead of gathering their bounty? Perhaps I should be grateful they are wasting time at my feeders and not planting more acorns on our green roof. Imagine a grove of oaks being on top of a crushed house in a hundred years.

I see them wrestling acorns off twiggy clusters of leaves and pounding them with their beaks. Do Scrub Jays ever reach a point when they know they have enough food and can slow down or even stop collecting more, at least for a while? That's a question I have of all birds that cache food. Or do they continue to hoard as long as supplies are present? Why not? They can't count on the human to be reliable. She might go off to New York or China again. A squirrel or another bird could steal their stash. A gale force wind could blow it away. Better steal from bird feeders as well.

It is winter now, and the Golden-crowned Sparrows come throughout the day and remain at the feeder to chow down. It took me a while to realize why they are voracious eaters. They are migrants, as are

FEEDING BEHAVIOR
non-breeding

JAN 7, 2020

Why are there so few oak titmice. Only three. Yet they were feeding an army of babies. Did most die or leave?

OAK TITMOUSE
Last year they were one of the most voracious eaters of mealworms — trying to carry four at a time. Now they take a seed to the tree & eat it. Come only a few times

Do male titmouse allow no other males in their territory?

DARK-EYED JUNCO
They ate a similar number of mealworms. There are many juncos. Perhaps juncos are socially in groups, whereas oak titmice are more territorial among their own. Is safety in numbers true?

the Townsend's Warblers and Fox Sparrows. They've flown in from thousands of miles away. They're famished when they arrive. They need energy to molt and pretty themselves up into fancy plumage. They need to store up reserves for the return to their northern homes in spring. Yet they can't gain too much weight. They would become slow flyers.

The tiny songbirds that nest and live here year-round don't come nearly as often as they did in the spring when they were feeding nestlings, but they continue to take food up to the trees, primarily the tiny suet balls the size of mints in a tin, which they can easily pinch-hold in their tiny beaks. They must be hoarding some of that suet in a tree cavity. The suspected hoarders are cavity nesters: titmice, chickadees, and nuthatches. How much can they stuff into a tree cavity? If suet balls are brimming over the top, would they simply find another cavity to stuff? When exposed to heat and rain, that greasy food isn't going to hold up well. I might be spending a fortune so birds can fill the cavities in five oak trees with moldy suet. I picture the tree cavity homes of nuthatches resembling the contents of my fridge when I've been out of town for long periods. *Oh, gross. What's that slimy green thing?*

VORACIOUS MIGRANTS

THEY ARRIVED HUNGRY AND NEVER
STOPPED EATING.

TOWNSEND'S
WARBLER

REMAINS ON
SUET UNTIL
BIGGER
BIRD
CHASES
IT AWAY

SUET
LOVER

I DON'T KNOW WHY IT TOOK ME SO
LONG TO REALIZE THE MIGRANTS EAT
THE MOST AT ONE SITTING. THEY
ARE STOCKING UP ON FAT, I'M GUESSING,
TO PREPARE TO MIGRATE BACK NORTH
THOUSANDS OF MILES AWAY. THAT'S
WHERE THEY NEST. WILL MY FEEDERS
MEAN MORE WILL SURVIVE THE LONG
JOURNEY?

January 14, 2020

The birds are freaking out. The chickadees set off the alarm, and other birds called out in a chorus of fear. I ran to the glass doors to see. Within a matter of seconds, the birds took off, including a hundred or so Lesser Goldfinches. There were so many one was driven into the wood railing. Until that moment, I thought we had only two dozen goldfinches at most.

Then I saw the reason for the panic: a hawk had swooped into the same oak tree that the goldfinches had fled. The hawk was bigger than a Cooper's Hawk. Its rich-brown coloration made me think it was either a Red-tailed or Red-shouldered Hawk, both of which are too big to bother with tiny chickadees and goldfinches that weigh a third of an ounce. Evidently the little birds also decided they were not on the menu. As the hawk moved about in the tree, some of the little songbirds returned, perched nearby, and continued their chatter. I thought the little birds were pretty smart to simply remain in the tree where a hawk wouldn't bother to eat them, and their mortal enemy, the Sharp-shinned Hawk, would not come close enough to try.

After resting for ten minutes, the hawk flew to a bare-branched tree, far enough away that some of the birds went down to the feeder again. I looked at the hawk through binoculars and also took photos. It looked downward most of the time, probably to scan the ivy for rats. I sent my little four-pound Yorkie mammal back into the house. He is too heavy for a hawk to carry away, but a Red-tailed Hawk can still injure a little dog by landing with talons. A Great Horned Owl, on the other hand, would have no problem carrying off my dog. I know of someone who had that happen to her Yorkie. I have heard the owls at dusk in our oak trees, Great Horned, by the sound of their hooting. I've never seen them. Nonetheless, I am cautious whenever I let the dogs out at night. They wear CoyoteVests with spikes over the back

14 JAN 2020

A HAWK PAYS A VISIT

WHICH? RED-TAILED OR RED SHOULDERED

EVERYONE HEAD TO ANOTHER TREE

IN A PANIC, ONE LESSER GOLDFINCH FLEW INTO A WOOD RAIL

ABOUT 25 LESSER GOLDFINCHES FLEW OUT OF THE OAK & FROM FEEDER

HAWKS LOVE ME!

WOW! BOBO! GO INSIDE!

I'LL KILL IT!

STOLEN SUET BALL

BOBO, FOUR POUND DOG

IT WAS A RED-SHOULDERED HAWK
IT LANDED ON A LIMB OF OAK. ALL BIRDS SCATTERED. THERE WERE MANY WARNING CRIES. HAWK WAGGED TAIL, LOOKING DOWN AT IVY BELOW. A RAT?

and neck and I am next to them. A dog with undulating silver spikes resembles a metallic porcupine. A rat would make a much better meal.

Later that night, after looking carefully at the photos I took of the hawk and those in a bird guidebook, I identified the raptor visitor as a Red-shouldered Hawk. The main field marks are the streaky light brown head, rufous shoulders, and the thin white barring across its rufous breast. It is less than half the size of a Red-tailed Hawk. Like most inexperienced birders, I can't judge size that well when out in the field. In the throes of excitement, I inflate the size. I am past the stage, however, when hawks become eagles, and turkey vultures become condors.

I am happy we have a Red-shouldered Hawk. It's a beauty. It won't hurt my dogs. The little birds aren't scared. Only the rats should worry.

March 9, 2020

We've been shut down by COVID-19, required to stay home. Almost everything seems like a potential transmitter of disease and death—the groceries, a doorknob, another person. But not the birds. The birds are balm.

I don't mind staying at home. I'm grateful to have a home with a yard, where birds are not aware that anything is amiss. They are too busy getting prepared for nesting season. I hear all kinds of birdsong today. The males are singing about their excellent genes. I used to think the Oak Titmice had just one call, a scratchy scolding sound. But now that spring is here, they've added courtship songs, ones that are melodically beautiful. One of them is loud and attention-grabbing. The mnemonic birders use to describe it is: "Peter! Peter! Peter!" What does that call mean? *"Hey, ladies, check me out. Fierce hunter of mealworms. Defender provider for you and babies. Does poop clean-up."*

I spotted an Oak Titmouse who has evidently found her mate. I knew it was a female because she was gathering materials for a nest, and only female titmice do the work. Because titmice mate for life, I wonder if she and her mate are among the Oak Titmice that nested in the yard last year. Today she came to the feeder stand where I had tied a twig ball filled with alpaca wool, a gift of our vet, Kathy. The titmouse pulled out a bit. At first, she seemed to be eating the wisps. She held it in her beak, and then using her foot, she drew the strands back and forth repeatedly. I guessed she might be testing the alpaca wool's tensile strength, fluffiness, and ability to withstand dampness. She approved and pulled at the wool ball fifteen or so times until she had a clump that looked almost as big as she was. She flew off looking like a little floating cloud. My eyes followed her to a large branch of the oak tree and then she disappeared into dense leaves. Likely she had already found a cavity deep enough for her nest, and it may not have been where I saw her land. Fluff is the finishing touch a titmouse uses to line the nest. The alpaca wool she collected means her nest is nearly done. She is just about ready to lay her eggs and will then brood for the next two weeks. After the chicks hatch, she and her mate will be busy bringing their nestlings food, including my prized suet balls and mealworms. And if all goes well, in another month, I may see this same titmouse bringing her fledglings to the mealworm feeders.

There is talk that the shutdown will continue into April. A lot can change. The pandemic may subside. In the meantime, I will never feel bored.

NESTING SEASON has started, as did THE SHUTDOWN

MARCH 9, 2020

An Oak Titmouse sat on the twig ball of llama's fur that Kathy G. gave me. She plucked some wool out and seemed almost to be eating it — testing its durability & ability to handle dampness? Satisfied she pulled out wool FIFTEEN TIMES then flew up to a branch in the oak tree. She must be almost done building her nest since lining it would take place at the end.

May 12, 2020

Four fluffy Oak Titmice fledglings came today, a wonderful sign that all the parents' efforts—and mine—to feed the nestlings mealworms have paid off. Only three days ago, these fledglings were fully dependent on their parents for food. Today I saw that these four are trying to figure out how to enter the cage with mealworms. But they still fly after the parent begging for food. One parent led the fledglings to a cage and secured a mealworm. The babies were all aflutter. Which one would be first to be fed? But the parent took off without giving the mealworm to any of them. The abandoned fledglings cried as they sat on different arms of the feeder station. Tough love.

Later in the day, a fledgling peered down into the cage feeder but stopped short of trying to enter. Sometimes it slid out of control down the curved arm of the feeder. Its parent returned and went into the mealworm cage five times to feed the fledge. If a baby can eat five mealworms in one sitting, how many must the parent retrieve to feed four babies throughout the day? When the adult took off, the fledge hesitated for a minute, clearly scared, before it flew to rejoin its parent. I think it will be only a matter of days before this fledgling will be forced to be on its own.

The baby titmice eat all day long—mealworms, mini suet balls, and sunflower chips. Their crop is always full, as it probably was when their parents fed them. Everything, including food sources, is new and I watched them investigate what is edible. One fledgling appeared shocked when the mealworm in its beak wiggled. Startled, the baby flung the mealworm into the air and watched it fall to the ground, like a human baby in a highchair. It took another from the bowl.

I read that the first three weeks after leaving the nest is a perilous time. Fledglings can easily starve or become prey if they do not learn

Parent
brings
five
mealworms
Is baby
grateful?

Godmother
Amy will
try to make
food easy
to find.

75% OF
BABIES
DIE
BEFORE
ADULTHOOD

In another few days,
this fledge will have to
fend for itself. Many
young birds starve.

enough from their parents in those first two weeks. Seventy-five percent don't survive to adulthood and of that number, 40 percent die in the first three weeks. To survive on their own, they must learn to dig around in branches for insects or even catch them as they fly by. I see them learning to do that in the trees. The mealworms will lessen the chances of their starving during the critical learning period. I position the patio umbrella so that the feeders and water bowls are not visible from the places where Cooper's and Sharp-shinned Hawks perch. I tell the little titmice a cautionary tale about a little bird that sat out in the open for twenty minutes wailing for its mama to come back, and only the hawk heard its cry. I tell them to not break my heart.

May 16, 2020

This morning, the yard was nearly deserted. It was as if the birds had also gone into lockdown. An empty yard always feels eerie, a sign of something sinister. In lieu of sweet birds hopping across the flagstone, three rats were checking out the rock crevices. The food bowls in the suspended cage feeders were empty. I added rounds of soft suet. After an hour, a few songbirds returned, then more of them, pairs of the Oak Titmice, Chestnut-backed Chickadees, Pygmy Nuthatches, Dark-eyed Juncos, California Towhees, Spotted Towhees, and Bewick's Wrens. They flew back and forth between the feeders and trees often. They must be feeding their nestlings. I looked in my nature journal from last year, and saw that by May 14, 2019, the birds were eating a combined total of 500–1,000 mealworms a day. I had no mealworms on hand, but I had plenty of suet. I smashed the suet into crumbles, which make it easy for the parent birds to quickly grab what they want without having to peck it into pieces. They all seemed to like this arrangement, and loaded up on suet crumbles until their crops were full and then they would pinch one more chunk to hold in their bills before ferrying this up to a nest—whereabouts unknown.

Lou drove me fifteen miles to Wild Birds Unlimited to buy live mealworms. I saw other customers there, all of us wearing masks. We don't greet each other. These are different times. Any of us could be carrying spiky RNA. We have all been cooped up for five weeks and this is a high moment. We obsessive bird lovers set on the counter the supplies we definitely need, and then continue to browse the new squirrel-proof bird feeders, the owl boxes, the books and binoculars, all kinds of things we don't need. In addition to sunflower chips, seeds, and suet, I decided my songbirds would love safflower seeds for variety. I bought more suet butter balls and also 5,000 live mealworms, which likely would not last a week. I can't buy more. I don't have enough room in the fridge to store them. Of course, I could buy another fridge for the garage. I have also contemplated starting my own mealworm farm. But doing either would be time-consuming and pathological. So I presented to the nine-year-old boy next door a business proposition, outlining how he could make a small fortune growing mealworms. I'd buy the supplies. He'd have a built-in customer base. Plus, I added, it would be fun for him to watch them grow. He would learn some really cool science. His mom did not agree.

CHESTNUT-BACKED
CHICKADEE
BACKYARD CHRONICLES
5-16-20

May 22, 2020

It's a warm day, and by design in consideration of the carbon footprint, we built a home without AC. To cool off, I push the bifold glass doors all the way open on both sides so that the main floor is like an open pavilion. The birds can fly in and out if they want. But I'm hoping they will be deterred by my presence at the dining table, which now serves as my pandemic office and viewing station.

One of the four baby titmice has become the leader. A few days ago, I noticed it was the first to arrive and stand at the top of the feeder station pole, calling for others with a scratchy *tsika-tsika*, followed by variations of other scolding sounds. When it leaned forward in position to fly, its siblings watched, and one leaned but shrank back. The leader leapt. *See, it's easy. I didn't die.* The siblings soon were comfortable enough to follow, one at a time. The leader made angry fast sounds when a sibling challenged it for food.

The baby titmice are now using the feeders, patio furniture, and fence like kids on a jungle gym. They fly from one elevation to another—from oak tree to fence, to the curved shepherd's hook, to the top of the patio chair, to the little swing dangling from a pole, which makes it a bridge of sorts for getting into the feeder. The leader is obvious because of its confidence. It uses fewer stopping points and can fly to a cage with enough accuracy to grab on to the bars. Will this titmouse remain the leader? Is that also how dominance starts? Is it smarter or stronger? Was it the first to leave the nest? Is it the bravest? What is bravery to a bird?

Mealworms are their favorite food and they can swallow four at a time, sucking them up like noodles. When they exit the cage, they often carry a spare mealworm up into the tree. A snack for dusk. When they first tried sunflower chips, they repeatedly dropped them, which meant, I am guessing, they were rejecting them. The seed's texture

5-22-20

HOW BABY BIRDS EXPLORE

TRY TO EAT
SOMETHING
TOO BIG

- PLAY FOLLOW
  THE LEADER
- JUMP FROM PLACE
  TO PLACE
- SLIP DOWN SHEPHERDS
  HOOK
- PEER INTO
  FEEDERS

BALANCE
ON
EVERYTHING

IS IT
ALIVE?

INVESTIGATE
THINGS THAT
MOVE AND
THINGS THAT
DON'T - BUT
MIGHT MOVE LATER

CALL FOR
PARENTS TO
BRING FOOD

must have seemed hard compared to the live and regurgitated meals stuffed into them by their parents.

One titmouse held the sunflower seed in its beak and tilted its head back in the feeding posture it used when its parent fed it. It evidently did not know how to open its bill to swallow. It simply let go of the seed. It then watched a nearby chickadee place a seed between its feet to jab at it and break it up into smaller, edible pieces. The titmouse immediately picked up the seed it had dropped and did the same!

I was amazed to see a baby bird learn by imitating the behavior of another species. The titmouse also watched a much larger bird, a California Towhee, jump into a flowerpot and poke around for food. The titmouse followed suit and discovered the flowerpot contained a large black seed of some sort, maybe the seed a Scrub Jay extracted from an acorn. It picked it up, and it barely fit in the cup of its fully opened mouth—way too big to swallow. It placed the seed between its feet and pecked at it, but had no success in cracking it open. It left the inedible seed and found suet in a bowl and easily broke off crumbs. I'm sure suet will become its favorite alternative when the mealworm bowl is empty.

I, too, am part of their curricula. The young birds have always seen me as part of the yard. I am the flightless animal that sits by the big glass doors and sometimes comes out. They associate me with the arrival of mealworms and make loud *tsika-tsika* sounds before I've even refilled the feeders. The titmice siblings wait at the top of the fence three feet away. The Chestnut-backed Chickadees, Bewick's Wrens, and Pygmy Nuthatches station themselves in the thin tree behind the fence. At first, they waited for me to leave before jumping down and entering the cages. But some are now acclimated to my presence and enter when I am still refilling the bowls.

Today, while I was seated at the table, a young titmouse flew into the big room. It reached a window on the other side, and I was relieved it did not crash. It pushed against the window and then simply lay limp at the bottom of the sill with its crest deflated, mouth open from stress, and tail feathers splayed out. I enclosed it with a paper towel, and it kept still as I carried it outside. It flew off as soon as I opened the paper towel. A few seconds later, it was back at the feeders, eating a seed while keeping an eye on me. *You're so brave,* I mouth to him.

Will the four titmouseketeers continue to visit the patio feeders together? Will they learn by their errant sibling's mistake to not fly into the house? When will they master the lovely *"peter-peter-peter"* tune the chicks' parents sang to them when their entire world was the interior of an eggshell?

May 31, 2020

Ravens do aerial acrobatics with other ravens for fun. Gulls take turns surfing. Crows slide down icy roofs. And in our yard, some of the songbirds use the little wire swing hanging off a shepherd's hook.

I watched a junco on a swing and was not sure it was play at first, since some birds use the swing as a stepping stone of sorts to maneuver their bodies into the mealworm cage. Birds also perch on it to wait their turn at the mealworm bowl. But by watching more closely, I saw how this junco, and later others, landed on the horizontal bar with enough force to set it in motion and deliberately thrust their chests forward to keep the swing going back and forth. They repeated this several times. One male junco started on the horizontal wooden bar and then switched to standing on the top of the swing's curved twisted wire. The junco kept pumping his chest out, but the swing would not move as it did when he stood on the lower bar. He abandoned his newfound toy.

The young titmice used the swing, at first, to get into the mealworm feeder. Their balance was wobbly, but they would deliberately go to the swing and stay on it for at least ten seconds as they assessed what to do next. Now they fly directly into the cage feeders, but they still take a short ride on the swing. The Pygmy Nuthatches and Chestnut-backed Chickadees also use the swing, although not as often. I only know this might be play when the bird swings and goes into the cage without taking food, and then hops back onto the swing to repeat the action. I think they discover by happenstance what in their expanding world is fun to do, just like I did as a kid wading through the creek. Part of the fun is discovering what's fun.

5.31.20

Used by juncos, chickadees titmice, pygmy nuthatch, and Anna's Hummer,

DARK-EYED JUNCO

Birds just wanna have fun

I was not sure at first if the birds were using the swing as a rest stop. But the more I watched how they deliberately jumped on, the more I was convinced this was play. They moved their bodies to enhance the swing motion.

June 13, 2020

I was once ambivalent in my appreciation of crows. Sure, they are smart and can astound with their problem-solving skills. They have huge and entertaining personalities. But they frighten the little songbirds and, if given a chance, would devour all the bird food, as well as eggs and baby birds in the nest. But today I watched a crow grooming and feeding three fledglings. It was endearing. I don't know if it was the mother, the father, or an older juvenile that tended to the fledglings. I read that all three may be involved in the care of the young. That right there is a reason to admire crows. A corvid's version of family values.

From reading, I know the crow fledglings are about 80 to 100 percent the size of adults. I noticed that the adult's stance is often more straight-legged, making them appear taller. The babies are easy to differentiate. Their bills are shorter than an adult's. They have blue eyes, pink gape flanges, and they scream like brats with bills wide open when they believe it is their turn to be groomed or fed, which is basically all the time. Given how competitive and demanding these young birds are, it is surprising that they later turn into a cooperative family group. At what point do the fledglings learn they are not the center of the world?

While being groomed, the fledglings extend their necks and remain still as the adult uses its bill to dig under feathers. Are the adults searching for mites or loose feathers? Is any of this grooming a parent crow's version of affection? What is human love if not feeding, cleaning, protecting, teaching, and tirelessly attending to the baby's other needs twenty-four hours a day? By that anthropomorphic model, crows, as well as all the birds I see, meet the behavioral criteria of demonstrating something that is at least akin to love. Or would a

biologist say that their caretaking behavior is innate and not attached to emotions?

The adults took the babies to the car park roof covered with gravel. This is the usual spot in our cul-de-sac of rooftops for teaching young birds to eat grit, the tiny pieces of rock, a few grades bigger than sand. I used to think birds were eating grit because they were starving—what a cruel world. I have since learned that grit in the bird's gizzard aids in digestion. "It's good for you," one can imagine the adult saying to her skeptical babies. I saw three blue-eyed baby crows testing the digestive aid. They picked up a bit in their bills and must have done a quick swipe with the tongue over the hard substance, before deciding it was too nasty to eat. They spit it out. Crows are smart, but like human children who must eat vegetables before dessert, these baby crows must learn to eat grit. Dessert, the adults promise, will be a raid on Amy's patio feeders.

TEACHING BABY CROWS   6·13·20
TO EAT GRIT

DON'T CAW
BACK AT ME!

I want
tourist
junk
food!

It's GOOD
FOR BIRDS!
GRIT IN THE
GIZZARD AIDS IN
GRINDING FOOD
PASSED IN DUAL
CHAMBERED STOMACH

Adult and fledgling crows.
  Standing on car park roof with gravel.
In the past, I've seen adults teaching
juveniles how to eat grit — good for
digestion. Today, I saw three
fledges testing gravel, but spitting it out.

July 16, 2020

It's hot again and the glass doors are pushed all the way to the side. Whenever I look out, I see the same mated pair of tubby California Towhees strolling across the patio, looking like landlords inspecting the premises for damages. They eat errant mealworms and sunflower seeds they find on the ground. Several times a day, they take baths in the biggest terra-cotta saucer or the turquoise bowl.

Towhees are sparrows, the largest of other sparrow species in our yard, 9" long, compared to the smallest sparrow, the Dark-eyed Junco, which is 5.75" to 6.5". One of this pair of towhees is bigger in girth and length than the other, and I assume it is the male. They stand on top of the square mealworm cage feeder I made, stick their heads in downward, and although it looks like it would be impossible for them to slip through the openings, one does, and eats heartily while smaller birds wait their turn.

I love drawing the angular head shape of the towhee. It juts up from the bill at a slight angle, and its crown is straight and flat before it slopes down a thick nape into the back. I learned from classes with John Muir Laws that a bird's head is not round, nor is its body from chest to belly. Follow the angles, the bone structure. And its plumage is not uniformly brown, as I discover when I draw detailed portraits. It is a rich combination of taupe, clay-gray, and rufous. The orange eyes are encircled by two or three rings of feathers, which resemble the eye bags of the sleep-deprived.

Birder friends have reported that towhees will walk into their home, inspect the rooms, and then saunter out. That hasn't happened here, although they have peered into the room when the bifold glass doors are open. Maybe they know a little dog is inside, and at eye level, he is a menace. I find almost everything about the towhee is comical. I love how it walks with a beer belly in a stately legato while the junco

7·16·20

MATED PAIR

CALIFORNIA
TOWHEE

They
dig by
Jumping
up on
both
feet
and kicking
backward,
sending
dirt flying.

A mated pair
are in the yard
most of the
day. They skip
into feeder from the
top. They drop meal-
worms into a flowerpot below,
then jump down, kick up dirt
and find the worms.

moves in pizzicato hops. I love its longing look when it cannot reach a tasty tidbit right away. I love its sudden burst of excitement while jumping and kicking dirt backward to roust the worms and insects. I love the way it pretends it is the king of ground feeders. I saw this same towhee slip into a mealworm cage feeder and drop mealworms into the flowerpot below. It then flew down to the flowerpot, kicked up dirt, and showed a sudden burst of excitement over its sham discovery. *Oh my, what's this? A worm?* Is that an avian version of make-believe? If it is doing this to impress a female, wouldn't that be false advertising? Or maybe a female would admire its trickery. I did.

CALIFORNIA
TOWHEE
IN THE BATH

July 28, 2020

Dusk is last call for the Anna's Hummingbirds. Dusk is the happy hour when two females will drink at the same feeder. Dusk is when I have seen two males—very young ones with short bills and molting raggedy feathers—occupying the same feeder as the graying sky takes on deeper, darker hues. The need is great to take in as much food as possible to last them through a night of a temporary hibernation-like state called torpor. I read that their heart rate slows from over 1,000 beats per minute to as low as 50. During daylight hours, they feed every 15 minutes, be it tiny insects or nectar from flowers or feeders. If they don't consume food often enough, they can die during the day. If they have not eaten enough before nightfall, they can die while asleep as they hang in suspended animation with tiny feet clutched to a thin branch.

Fiona said that if you touch a hummingbird in torpor, it will not wake up. A predator could easily consume it in a bite. When they come out of torpor, they're like me, requiring 15–30 minutes to come to wakefulness and fuel up, me with coffee, them with nectar or insects. In my yard, I have both nectar feeders and flowering plants, no matter what the season. I have five hummingbird feeders on different sides of the house. Plastic red ones, utilitarian and easy to clean. I put the smaller feeders in areas that are more hidden from direct view of the main patio flyway, and because many hummingbirds like the secret watering holes, those feeders drain quickly. The big feeder that is out in the open is the battleground for the males. Hummingbirds are more territorial than any of the other species in the yard. Right now, they're not just fighting over the nectar, they are fighting over the ladies.

The other day, I witnessed two flashy-headed male hummers in a chase. One drove off the other, and then the victor settled on a feeder. A pale green female joined him. The male drank heartily, and the female simply watched him chug down the nectar for at least a minute. She did not take a single sip. Not that he offered. Among Anna's Hummingbirds, there is no egalitarianism. Would the namesake Anna have approved? When the female slowly rose and took off, he followed, perhaps to the wedding bough where she will splay herself. I have no idea what she saw in him over others. Not long ago, I would have called them a mated pair. But that implies they mate and stick together like a married couple. Then I read that hummingbird males, despite all their courtship dazzle and battle, don't stick around after their mission is accomplished, which takes all of about four seconds. The males are deadbeat dads that contribute nothing to making the nest, or to feeding either the female or the nestlings. They are off to find other females they can impress with their deep dives, chasing skills, and commandeering of feeders.

A few days ago, in the late afternoon, one male hummingbird came to the feeder I was holding. He was young, to judge by his relatively short bill and scruffy feathers. He regarded me for a few seconds and then settled on the feeder. His need for food before torpor was probably greater than his caution of me. Because the liquid in the feeder was low and his bill was shorter than an adult's, his tongue could not reach the remaining liquid in the feeder. So I tilted it toward him and he drank for a good long while. Tonight, I again tried to lure hummers to the feeder held in my hand. A female came to the feeder, but just as she settled down, another hummingbird chased her off. A male, of course.

If I were a more diligent birder, I would get up at 6 a.m. to lure the hummingbirds for breakfast. Instead, I'll try again tomorrow for last call at dusk, a glass of red wine in one hand and a red feeder in the other.

JULY 28, 2020

ANNA'S HUMMINGBIRD

At dusk, I saw two females drink at the same patio feeder. Later, a male + female. The F. watched

last call at the bar. This is the magic hour of DUSK when the hummers must have their fill for the night. They are more willing to drink from the feeder held in my hand. One young hummer (shorter bill, less vibrant coloring) had a hard time reaching the nectar, so I tilted the feeder and he drank happily. Adult males initially tried to chase me from feeder before settling.

September 1, 2020

The wildfire smoke brought in another new bird. Using John Muir Laws's ID technique, I quickly said aloud what I saw: "Gray head, rufous breast, bigger than a towhee"...and then it flew away. But soon another bird took its place. It was mostly soft gray, and very fat. I looked through binoculars and saw a round dark eye and white eye ring, a decurved sharp beak. A Hermit Thrush? The beak was a little short for a Hermit Thrush. I decided it was another species, to judge by the white spots instead of darker ones on its breast. I was able to take a few photos, and when I looked at them later, I saw this little dumpling had blue upper feathers. Could it possibly be... a Western Bluebird fledgling? I have seen adults in open terrain in the Marin Headlands, sitting on jutting rocks along the crest of the coastal mountains. That is the bluebird's habitat, and not my woodland setting of four oak trees and a roof garden of succulents. Both birds lacked the bright blue and rufous breast I associate with bluebirds. But that duller coloration matched a female bluebird, and beside her, a pale offspring. Fledglings, I find, are so hard to identify, unless you see another bird of its kind next to it. None of my guidebooks show illustrations of fledglings, only juveniles. So there's an idea for someone: an illustrated book of fledglings, day one through ten.

The question is, why did Western Bluebirds come to my yard? Are they, too, affected by the ongoing wildfires up north? Serial wildfires have been burning since August, one after the other, ignited by lightning or sparking electrical wires, or evil arsonists. Since 2017, California has been burned and singed nonstop, it seems. The Southern Marin Fire Department tells us we should be prepared in our own town because it is not a question of *if* but *when*. Is the smoke worse in the Headlands? Maybe it is less. When there is heavy fog in Sausalito, our area, the Banana Belt, is usually fog-free. Would the Banana Belt

9-1-20

WILDFIRE SMOKE
BRINGS NEW
VISITORS.
First,
a thrush
of some kind.

WESTERN
BLUEBIRD
Mom and
baby

It sat on
the shepherd's
hook and
looked around,
then left.
But soon it returned with a dumpling of
a bird. The baby fledgling has blue
peeking through its creamy taupe feathers.
I knew what it was, I see them up
in the Headlands, in open terrain.

effect apply to smoke? Is heavy smoke the reason I have seen four new species in the last three weeks? The birds must be coming here to breathe and bathe. Some are molting. They need to clean off the soot and rid themselves of loose feathers to stay in top aerodynamic form. Amy's spa offers a choice of terra-cotta saucers filled with fresh water. I tell the birds: *Alaskan taste, fresh from globally warmed glacier melt.* I have seen these new birds put a tentative toe in the water, and I do think they are assessing depth with unfamiliar water sources and not temperature. When they enter the birdbath, they sit with breast and belly immersed. They dunk their head and flap. Often, they stay for at least a minute or two, sometimes even longer. This is when they are great subjects to sketch. But they are also sitting ducks, vulnerable to being taken by a Cooper's Hawk or a Sharp-shinned. I have seen hawks on occasion. I don't begrudge them their meal. Many raptors starve. But please don't take that baby bluebird that just looked me in the eye.

October 12, 2020

Battle at the birdbath! The scene: six terra-cotta saucers and one plastic turquoise bowl. I fill to a depth of an inch to an inch and a half, and place a rock in each one so that arriving migrants know immediately that the water depth is safe. I watch the new visitors standing on the rim of the birdbath, then dipping a tentative toe to feel bottom. The regulars are savvy and jump right in. I've heard sorrowful tales from friends and family who found a pretty bird that had sung to them earlier in the day, drowned later in a fountain deep enough to bathe a dog. Songbirds can't swim like ducklings. Before I knew much about birds, I never would have considered that. The style of the fountain would have been more important.

I fixed my binoculars on the largest terra-cotta saucer, currently the most popular. It started with the usual squabbles. An immature White-crowned Sparrow with rufous brows stood tall, staring at a Golden-crowned Sparrow that was submerged and soaking wet, a vulnerable spot to be in. I'm puzzled that birds that are so skittish out in the open for even a few seconds are less wary in a birdbath for three minutes. Along came another White-crowned Sparrow, an adult with vivid black brows and a stark white crown. All three left. Why didn't one stay? A Golden-crowned Sparrow took advantage and chased off two other Golden-crowned that were about to jump in. But when a Hermit Thrush stepped into the bath, the Golden started a smoldering stare down. Neither of them backed off. The Hermit stood tall on its long legs, towering over the seated Golden. It then lowered itself into the bath and splashed its wings vigorously. In turn, the Golden furiously flapped its wings. I was reminded of kids at a public pool who splashed others until they made them cry. Just when I thought they had achieved detente, they both went into simultaneous and vigorous wing-flapping, which went on for several minutes, an exhausting expenditure of their energy. The song from *Annie Get Your Gun* came to mind: "Anything you can do, I can do better."

To the casual human observer, it may appear the birds are bathing cooperatively and as equals. From watching the birdbath scene today, I am guessing that birds are more driven to establish dominance over the bath among their own kind. The dominant bird might share, but the subservient bird must look away. That behavior serves as a clue to me which bird is deferential. Those subtle behaviors of dominance and subservience are always in play. More migrants are returning and using the birdbaths, so there are more occasions for dominant birds to show the newcomers who controls the waterfront real estate.

From where I sit, I can see the birds splashing. Water goes flying, and by the end of the day, the birdbaths will be half-empty. The popularity of my birdbaths feels like the reciprocation of love.

October 20, 2020

I was horrified to see a half-dozen yellow jackets in a cage feeder chewing on live mealworms. The mealworms in turn were squirming, extending themselves upward like sun-seeking bean sprouts. Do mealworms feel pain? I don't want to assume a Descartesian logic that mealworms can't reason, and therefore don't feel pain. Who has the research on this?

The birds avoided the cage after seeing the bowl occupied by yellow jackets. I put another bowl on the ground that the birds could easily get to. Yellow jackets seem to prefer dining higher up. I used to worry that the birds might get stung and suffer serious injury. But I read that their feathers protect them. I have skin. I had to protect myself by dousing peppermint oil on my head, my hands, and other exposed areas. Yellow jackets dislike mint. The birds seem indifferent to the scent. I once thought birds weren't able to smell or taste, which would account for why birds aren't bothered by capsicum in suet, whereas squirrels are so disgusted they no longer visit the feeders. But I read recently that birds do indeed have olfactory receptors and taste buds, albeit fewer than mammals do. And so do yellow jackets. They can smell *Eau de Picnic* from a mile away.

I considered whether to get rid of the yellow jackets. Like bees, yellow jackets are pollinators, and the world is suffering a loss of those. Our rooftop garden is designed for bees, butterflies, and birds, so there are many critters that help with pollination. I got a couple of yellow jacket traps and was happy to learn they do not lure honeybees. I made an irresistible concoction of sugar and raw dog food, added water, and hung the trap next to the mealworm feeder. Immediately several yellow jackets went inside. They buzzed around a bit, and when they slipped down the side and landed in the soup, they struggled to stay afloat. Two tried to climb on top of the chunks of dog food, which

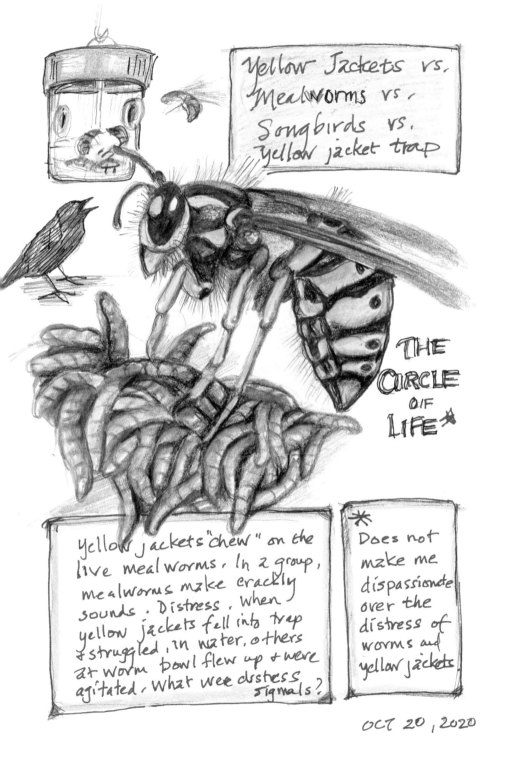

Yellow Jackets vs.
Mealworms vs.
Songbirds vs.
Yellow jacket trap

THE
CIRCLE
OF
LIFE*

Yellow Jackets "chew" on the
live mealworms. In a group,
mealworms make crackly
sounds. Distress. When
yellow jackets fell into trap
& struggled, in water, others
at worm bowl flew up & were
agitated. What were distress
signals?

* Does not
make me
dispassionate
over the
distress of
worms and
yellow jackets

OCT 20, 2020

rotated like a log in a river. I felt bad. They wanted to live. They must have been signaling their distress because all the yellow jackets in the mealworm restaurant just inches away flew out and circled the yellow jacket trap in a buzzing frenzy. I read somewhere that yellow jackets can recognize each other by their faces. I wondered if those outside the trap recognized the ones who were drowning. What were their would-be rescuers communicating. *Zzzz! Zzzz! Zzz!* Translation: *Hang on, Stella, we're working on a plan.* The would-be rescuers carefully crawled around on the exterior toward the opening, but then, as if spooked, they flew away. Were the drowning yellow jackets emitting a warning to stay away and save themselves? Do yellow jackets behave altruistically, as some ant colonies do?

I don't feel indifferent to any creature struggling to survive. I think my distress over theirs is a good thing.

October 27, 2020

Every day I refill the two feeders on the verandah with unshelled hot pepper sunflower chips. A gang of Lesser Goldfinches empties them, tossing most of the seeds on the ground before selecting one. They can also half empty the sock of Nyjer I hung off the shepherd's hook, leaving half the contents below. In days of yore, before I bought the pepper-laced stuff, the squirrels would eat up the mess. But now the squirrels have decided my feeders have bad juju. They stay away from the feeders. There is so much mess due to the finches, even the ground-feeder birds cannot eat it up fast enough. That leaves plenty for legions of rats, unless I sweep up the mess every evening. Then only two or three rats show up.

I asked Bernd Heinrich if he knew why feeder birds, like finches, discard so many seeds. It turns out he and other scientists did research on this back in the 1990s—of course, he did—measuring discarded seeds with painstaking accuracy. The short answer: Songbirds prefer shorter, fatter unshelled sunflower seeds, more depth than length, because they contain more oil. They take half a second to judge the seeds, dropping the low-density ones, until they find a seed to their liking. It is not unlike my thumping a watermelon to assess density as a factor in sweetness, only I don't throw the rejected melons on the store floor. According to Bernd, these oily seeds provide more energy than the long flat ones, so it's worth expending the energy to fly great distances for oil-rich food. The thing is, my feeders are only twenty feet away from the branches where the birds lallygag around. So I don't cut the finches any slack for tossing out perfectly good seeds and making a mess. They are not being nutritionally efficient. They're just slobs.

Today I removed the feeder they emptied the fastest and swept up the seeds, which were in perfect condition. I placed these in a small terra-cotta saucer and then set that within a larger saucer, which created an empty moat. Amazingly, the Lesser Goldfinches immediately took to this arrangement. Up to six at a time sat on the rim of the bigger saucer and ate the rejected seeds in the smaller saucer. They dropped rejected seeds, bits of shells, and the skins in the moat. When a seventh goldfinch tried to join in, the others drove it off. Now, whenever a goldfinch rejects a seed, the seed remains in the saucer. The birds were like reformed shoppers who have learned to put rejected fruit back in the bin.

With bird feeders, mess management and marauding rats will remain a work in progress. For now, I deserve a trophy for outsmarting the squirrels.

A. B. C. D. E. F.

A STUDY OF BIRD FEEDER ERGONOMICS AND WASTE

OCT 27, 2020

October 30, 2020

I saw a tiny bird with a streaky body on the feeder on my office porch. I remained still. Its beak was thin. After an absence of two years, the Pine Siskins have returned to my yard. I am remembering now an irruption of Pine Siskins that occurred three years ago. A salmonellosis epidemic broke out and there were reports of dead Pine Siskins littering many backyards. I saw only one sick Pine Siskin, which I am sure died soon after. I was heartsick and took down all the feeders for many months. And now I look at this delicate bird with dread. The problem is, they are a chummy species. They hang out together, eat together, and use the same bath and drinking water. If one individual is sick, disease can quickly spread to others, usually other finches. They are a model for how COVID-19 spreads. They do no social distancing and come together in large gatherings. With epidemics, they die in the wild or at the feeders. Fortunately, their food preference is the same. The finches eat only seeds. They take no interest in suet that the other birds favor.

All the finches in my yard sit for long periods munching away on seeds. They all do this—the House Finch, Lesser Goldfinch, American Goldfinch, Purple Finch, and Pine Siskin. I do the same with sunflower seeds in the shell, cracking them open until the tip of my finger used to pry open the shell is sore. Lou complains that I make a big mess. So who am I to criticize the finches? But my discards are just inedible shells. I am not wasteful with the seeds.

The goldfinches sometimes fight with each other at the feeder, beak to beak, and in the summer, the larger ones with brighter yellow plumage tend to win. Is there correlation between most vivid plumage and dominance? I seem to ask that question a lot about all kinds of birds.

When I first started noticing birds, I did not recognize any finch species in my yard. Eventually I saw yellow birds and learned they

American Goldfinch
and
Pine Siskin
10. 30. 20

were goldfinches, but I could not differentiate an American Goldfinch from a Lesser Goldfinch, or a Purple Finch from a House Finch. These days I can identify them all, adults and juveniles, and even when they are in winter garb, and not their more dazzling summer wear. Right now the American Goldfinches are warm beige over their backs and wings, and the Lesser Goldfinches are more olive yellow.

The goldfinches, for the most part, leave the smaller Pine Siskins alone when both are at the feeder. I saw only one squabble between a Pine Siskin and a Lesser Goldfinch. The Pine Siskin won, that is, it remained at the feeder and on the perch of choice. That's impressive. The feisty Pine Siskin is smaller. That goes against my previous observation that size determines dominance. I am always happy to find exceptions to what I hastily judged to be the rule. Nature abhors a generalist.

Lesser
Goldfinch

November 24, 2020

When I saw my first Townsend's Warbler a couple of years ago, I thought it would be a one-off bird. It was so striking, so different, and a warbler. When I saw another the next day, my heart took flight. Another rare sighting. Now, whenever I look out the bathroom window, I see the bandit-faced Townsend's Warbler in the round suet feeder two feet away. They are a reliable bird, a satisfying bird, there first thing in the morning, and among the last birds to visit the feeders before dark. In fact, when they first arrived they visited almost all of the fifteen different feeders, even the ones for the hummingbirds, which contain nothing more than sugar water. The warbler is also the only bird that uses the clear plastic open feeder, a round bowl with a wide moat for holding suet. It has a large clear dome to protect the contents from rain. Any bird can easily obtain food from it. But even the Scrub Jay won't touch it. My guess is that the birds are spooked by the big clear dome. So why isn't the Townsend's Warbler bothered by it? And why does it check out all the feeders? Is this driven by a migrant bird's need to find all available food sources before their return to their home turf thousands of miles away? Is it comparable to humans checking out every dish at the "all-you-can-eat" buffet? Skip the fruit salad in mayo, take the smoked salmon.

Lucky for me, the feeder the warbler visits most often now is still the one by my bathroom window. It is suspended from a shepherd's hook by the camellia bush and windowsill, where many birds hang out. Every morning I throw seeds on the ledge and hope the little birds eat it before the rats or Scrub Jays do. Every day I stand at the sink, brushing my teeth, a spectator to endless dramas and comedies that set the tone for what might otherwise be an ordinary day in pandemic times.

11·24·20

"the dabbler"

TRIES
EVERY
FEEDER

round
cage feeder

suet
feeder

suet
cage
feeder

JOWNSEND'S
WARBLER

OPEN DOME
PLEXIGLAS
FEEDER

seed
feeder

November 26, 2020

I was tardy in sorting a fresh shipment of 6,000 mealworms into containers. They sat in the extra fridge in the guest studio. For thirty-six hours, the birds looked in the bowls, confused that there were no live mealworms. They had to make do with suet cakes, suet balls, sunflower seeds, millet, Nyjer, safflower seeds, and butter bark—meaning, nobody should feel sorry for them. I used to fill four bowls with mealworms. That was incredibly time-consuming—and expensive. I cut down to one bowl and I refill as needed, which amounts to around 1,000 a day. I rationalize the cost of mealworms by calculating the amount of money I have saved by not having children. I would have been funding college tuition for grandkids by now. I can justify buying mealworms by the millions.

When I finally filled the bowl with mealworms today, the first customer was one of the Hermit Thrushes I regularly see in the yard. Its long thin legs make it appear fragile. It entered the cage immediately and gobbled down one mealworm every five seconds. I counted the seconds down. The mealworms were wiggling like mad, very much alive when the Hermit nabbed them. I watched carefully to see if it pulled on the mealworm until it snapped in two. That's what some of the juvenile birds do. They are disconcerted when their food wiggles. This Hermit Thrush was a pro. It swallowed them live and whole, sucking them in like soba noodles. I've seen many songbirds eat five, six, or even seven at a time. But this Hermit Thrush ate fifteen. When it stopped, it did not fly off, as most birds do after eating. It stood perfectly still. I wondered if it felt sick from overeating. Then its belly started undulating from side to side like a belly dancer. I pictured a clump of fifteen still-live mealworms roiling inside. Could it feel the mealworms crawling inside? Where in the digestive tract were the

11-26-20 THANKSGIVING

Early bird gets
the worm —
15 of them!

A
Thanksgiving
Tale of
Stuffing a Bird

Help!

Mercy

I was dilatory in
refilling the containers
with the shipment of
6000 mealworms. The
birds had only suet
to eat for a day & half.
Poor birds! Today when I finally filled
a bowl with mealworms, the first
to arrive was a Hermit Thrush—
Clearly experienced, it downed 15
worms — wriggling live ones,

mealworms? Still in the crop? How soon did the mealworms cease moving?

I did find a possible answer to the belly dance movement. Birds have dual-chambered stomachs. They push down the food in the crop into the chamber with digestive juices. The other chamber contains the gizzard, along with grit, which grinds the food. Perhaps the Hermit's undulations related to pushing the mealworms down from the crop, or it was sloshing them back and forth between the two chambers. The Hermit Thrush stopped its belly dance after a few seconds and flew off.

I have 12,000 mealworms left to sort. The task of shaking them out of wadded newspapers and putting them into containers has become more tolerable. But I can still feel them squirming, trying to escape. They don't have voices, but I imagine them giving warning to others through some means, contortions or by rubbing their bodies together, which produces a sizzling sound. Into the fridge they go, and as the cold settles into their bodies, the sizzling stops, and they are dormant. In twelve days, the birds will have devoured all of them. At that point, I will discontinue feeding mealworms until nesting season in the spring. Let them eat suet cake.

11-26-20

Since the worms were squirming as
the Hermit
Thrush ate
them in a gulp,
I started to
wonder if the
worms were
still alive
in the gullet
or stomach.
Just as
I thought
this, the
HETH moved
its belly side
to side, as if
the mealworms
had caused, this
to happen. When
the action stopped,
the HETH left.

Hermit
Thrush

side-to-side
movement
of belly

So what was that belly action? A
way to settle the mealworms? Does it
aid in digestion - Was it discomfort?
Do birds get bellyaches from overeating?

December 9, 2020

As I had predicted, the Pine Siskins that arrived five weeks ago have brought along their friends and relatives. There were flocks of twenty, and soon a cloud of them. I now estimate there are over a hundred. They squabble and fight off other birds and their own kind for seed rights. They discard half the seeds and make a huge mess, which, as usual, the quail, ground feeders, and rats appreciate.

This week, the large number of Pine Siskins in the yard has attracted the attention of hawks. Several times a day, the yard will empty all at once. Often a chickadee is the first to cry out an alarm. Chatter crescendos, followed by a mass exodus and silence. When this happens, I scan the nearby oak trees and usually spot the reason, a Cooper's Hawk on one occasion, and a Red-shouldered Hawk on at least two other occasions. Songbirds are on the menu for a Cooper's Hawk. The eatery for a Red-shouldered Hawk lies right below its talons: the neighbor's overgrown ivy patch, where rats live in a paradisal metropolis of burrows, damp dirt, rotting leaves, mold, mildew, fungus, and insects. The hawk's head bobbed as it looked downward. Its tail did stiff wags. I read that the hawk's head bob may be a way to calculate the distance to prey—sort of like my camera lens moving back and forth as I focus on my subject, in this case, the Red-shouldered Hawk. The tail wag, I read, is also part of a hawk's hunting behavior. Is it a functional movement, like getting the rudder of a plane in place? Does the sideways wag waft the air and give it lift? Or is it simply an expression of the hawk's excitement in seeing a potential meal? The hawk eventually jumped down to another limb in a leisurely manner and then flew out of sight. My yard is where the hawks and the songbirds meet, one as diner, the other as dinner. I try to not root for one over the other.

MIGRANT SONGBIRDS — A
SEASONAL DIET FOR HAWKS

RED-
SHOULDERED
HAWK

PINE SISKIN
4.5" - 5.25"
RED-
SHOULDERED
HAWK
16" - 32"

12·9·20

Among the migrants, the
Pine Siskin (PISI) is the
most numerous — at least
a hundred. They clog the
feeder, scare up into
clouds. The large
number of feeder birds
may be why we are
seeing more hawks.
This Red-Shouldered
Hawk (RSHA) has
come at least twice—
likely daily.

As the hawk scouted
the yard for food,
its tail did a stiff wag, and
it bobbed its head. The head
bob may be an attempt to hone in
on prey off in the distance, sort of
like adjusting the camera to
capture the hawk. Alas, no luck.

PINE SISKIN
sits on the long
feeder perch a long
time, making them
easy prey.

January 17, 2021

On this beautiful Sunday at home, we sat on the verandah with friends, enjoying an outdoor meal. We are following COVID-safe protocols, our tables being ten feet apart, each table with its own takeout food, along with pump bottles of hand sanitizer. We provided guest binoculars to spot boats on the bay and birds in the sky. Those will be disinfected later.

The birds seem to be enjoying the sunny day as much as we are. An immature Red-tailed Hawk flew leisurely past us at eye level. Two Scrub Jays and two Steller's Jays—a bird rarely seen in my yard—posted themselves like sentinels in separate naked birch trees and chatted just before leaving and joining up with others of their own kind. Our friend John, head of a conservation organization, used to work for Point Blue when it was still known as the Point Reyes Bird Observatory. He is a good spotter and listener. He pointed to a tree about fifty yards away. "Two woodpeckers," he said. "Do you hear them?" I heard nothing. He said they were making knocking sounds back and forth, and that perhaps they were a male and female.

I have been losing my hearing, and if there was any incentive for me to get a hearing aid, listening to birdsongs was it. He pointed to two hummingbirds that were rising together in close formation. The hummingbirds usually chase each other, but this was probably a male courting a female. The hummingbirds and owls tend to start nesting early in the year. I am hearing more birdsong in closer proximity, the impressive kind heard in the spring. The most exciting was listening to a Great Horned Owl *hoo-hoo*ing as dusk fell.

In the bushes and low trees by the patio, I saw two Western Bluebirds, a Spotted Towhee, two Oak Titmice, a half-dozen Golden-crowned Sparrows, Anna's Hummingbirds, Chestnut-backed Chickadees, Townsend's Warblers, Hermit Thrushes, California Towhees, Bewick's

Jan 17, 2021
Sunday 70°

GOLDEN-
CROWNED
SPARROW

Sheltering
in
Place

OAK TITMOUSE

ANNA's
HUMMINGBIRD

The birds all use
the same bushes and
low trees for reconnaissance
—to look up for predators,
to rest between turns at the
feeder, to see what others
are doing, to watch me. ~

Wrens, Dark-eyed Juncos, White-throated Sparrows, Ruby-crowned Kinglets, and Pygmy Nuthatches. They all seem to use the same bushes and trees to do reconnaissance, to check the sky for predators, to survey food on the patio, to watch others of their own kind, and to rest a minute or two between eating. Just now, a couple of Townsend's Warblers shot out of the canopy of the oak tree by the verandah and quickly returned. They are catching insects in mid-air, John said.

Thanks to the birds, I have never felt cooped up staying at home. So much remains new, so much can be discovered. As restricted as we are by the specter of a deadly disease, when watching birds, I feel free.

Townsend's Warbler (female)

January 18, 2021

I hear it singing before I see it, a very cheerful song. And then, there it is, the White-throated Sparrow. The mnemonic people usually go by to learn its song is "Old-Sam-Peabody-Peabody-Peabody." So boring, and who are Sam and Peabody? I would change the song to something more appropriate for courtship: "I'm-here-take-a-look-take-a-chance-take-a-mate." They have visited from time to time, and now one has stayed longer than a couple of days. I might even call it a regular. It is slightly larger than the Golden-crowned Sparrows. Both are ground feeders, but the White-throated has proven to be the most aggressive of the sparrows in claiming the suet cage feeder. Other birds watch it slip into the cage, grab a suet ball, and exit. But it stands just inches away from the cage to eat and then goes back into the cage. Why does it get out of the cage at all? Is it deliberately luring birds to go in so it can assert itself? It's like the big kid that says to the little kid, "Take it. I dare you." It charges any bird that dares—all but the California Towhee, which is the biggest sparrow of the yard, and more of a big goofball than a bully. But might is right. There are probably scores of ways that birds display their status. If I take slo-mo video, would I see more of them, those combinations of wing flicks, head turns, eye contact, raised brow and crests, and posture adjustments? I want to understand the language of birds. What are they saying about me?

WHITE-CROWNED SPARROW
RULES THE FEEDERS

1·18·21

WAITLIST:
GCSP
DEJU.
BEWR

WHITE-
THROATED
SPARROWS
RULE

GOLDEN
CROWNED
WAITS

Sometimes a
GCSP will
grab a
suet ball
that fell out
of the bowl.

A big rush for the
suet balls in the cage feeder. The
white-throated Sparrow appears and
the other birds leave. Sometimes, they
dip a beak in and snatch a suet
ball. The GCSP behind the WTSP is
in breeding plumage and is King of
the GCSP, but a lacky to the WCSP.

January 27, 2021

Because it was raining, I took down the suet cage feeder and set it on the patio right next to the glass bifold door. I covered it with a black protective rain tarp but left it open a few inches at the bottom, so I could peer in. I lay on my stomach and my face was about six inches from the food bowl, separated only by glass. Would a bird driven by a need for food overcome caution and eat with a human so close by?

Are birds sensitive to barometric pressure fluctuations? They will eat in a frenzy right before it rains and also when it stops, even momentarily. Maybe they are frantic because the flying insects that make up a lot of their diet are hunkered down with their sodden wings during the storm. Maybe birds are like humans during a pandemic who, when confronted with the possibility that they will run out of toilet paper, will buy enough for ten years. Only with excess do they feel secure. The birds do, in fact, cache excess food, most of which, I imagine, simply rots. Damp green suet with its own acquired life forms. Do birds have an innate need to store as much as they can in the winter? Which birds store food and which don't? I am guessing ground feeders don't since they don't live in trees. Can birds also tell if food is spoiled?

A few birds hopped up close to the cage but did not go in. A Townsend's Warbler came by briefly, followed by a Bewick's Wren. Both are equally small. I've noticed that the smallest birds in my yard tend to be the least intimidated by me. The ones who come near me by a foot or less have probably been here long enough to know I bring food and cannot fly and chase them. I talk softly to them when they land near me. *You're so brave.*

The Bewick's Wren entered the cage I had placed next to the glass door. It was watching me as intensively as I was watching it as it ate just inches from my face. It appeared by its smooth and evenly taupe

1-27-21

CLOSE ENCOUNTERS
with a BEWICK'S WREN

cage feeders I built

Wore my camo top to blend in.

When it started raining, I put the bird feeders under the umbrella on the patio table, all but one, which I placed next to the glass door. I crouched down on the other side of the glass. Eventually, a BEWICK'S WREN came in and I watched it eat soft suet. Surprise! It draws it up into its tongue.

Like a hummingbird's tongue!

suet

It was aware I was there. I think birds understand that when I don't move and am inside, I am not a threat.

plumage to be an adult, and thus, experienced at assessing danger, opportunity, and reward. It probably knew its escape routes. It does not know that I can hardly breathe as I watch. *Please don't leave.*

Its bill is slightly curved and proportionally long and thin compared to, say, a sparrow's. It poked at the suet, and then, it did something I have never seen other birds do, except for a hummingbird. With its bill seemingly closed, it stuck out its thin tongue to draw the food in. Is that why it favored crumbly suet? What other birds do this? Finches grab seeds between their beak and bite down slightly to loosen the thin skin of the seed before using their tongue to bring the de-skinned seed into their open mouths, still chomping with their open beaks as the food moves back toward their crop. Juncos and Oak Titmice peck at suet, break it up into manageable pieces, and then with mouth open draw in the crumbs. There may be many birds that keep their bills closed and stick out the tongue to draw in food. What does a woodpecker do after it drills into the suet? It has an incredibly long tongue for sticking into crevices.

Being up close and personal allows me to see behavior I would not have noticed otherwise. And although birds will come to hanging cages while I am standing in front of them, they don't tarry, unlike the Bewick's Wren in this novel arrangement. Perhaps the Bewick's Wren knows that the glass between us prevents me from reaching it. If that is the case, what cognition enabled this wren to discern that? Other feeder birds seem to know that when I am standing still behind the glass door, I am not a threat. But if I move, I am.

I am tempted to call this wren brave. But in humans, it involves a disregard for safety combined with selflessness that overrides fear—a character trait many admire. I once saw a male Crowned Lapwing on safari in South Africa fly up in front of the vehicle feigning a broken wing to draw attention away from the female sitting on a gravel nest with three eggs on the side of the road. Killdeer do this too. Was that behavior simply instinct without intention to be altruistically brave? If it is instinct, it might be driven by the need to ensure the survival of the female sitting on the eggs that will be its progeny. I keep running into these questions about instinct and intention in birds. Instincts, like those related to migration, can be scientifically verified repeatedly. Trying to figure out a bird's intentions runs afoul of anthropomorphism. I cannot possibly know what a bird's intentions are. How do I know what it needs? I remind myself that the guesses are only that. Yet I still can't help wanting to know what is really going on. It's like what I do with fiction. One character's intentions and what another wants to believe are the beginning of a story, always subject to change.

BEWICK'S
WREN

February 7, 2021

I found a few downy feathers in one of the terra-cotta water bowls. The pooh-bahs in Facebook bird groups would immediately yell in cap letters to leave the feathers where I found them, that it is a federal offense to do anything with wild bird feathers. I rinsed out the water bowls, sending most of the fluff into the dirt of the jasmine planter box. I took one bit of down inside so I could later draw it and study how it differs from fully shafted feathers with stiff barbules. But then I misplaced the fluff, and the evidence of my felonious feather gathering was gone. I will not go to prison, a place where I could have gotten a lot of writing done.

The fluff in the water bowls was probably from the Golden-crowned Sparrows. They are bathing more often now that they are molting into full breeding plumage—black brows, neon yellow crown, gray cheeks. I used to wonder why some of them remained taupe colored with brown brows. Were they females? No, I learned, females have breeding plumage identical to the males and do not look different. I then read that first-winter birds (birds going through their first winter) will not be ready to breed for another year. So those taupe-colored Goldens could be either male or female immatures.

I feel like I am missing out on a lot of Golden-crowned Sparrow behavior by not being able to tell males from females. One source said that females are possibly smaller. I mentioned that to another birder expert and received a quizzical look, which means whoever told me that was misinformed. But in doing sketches of the Goldens at the water bowl or on the windowsill, I do see variation in size. eBird describes the Goldens as being 7" in length. I am guessing the ones in my yard range between 6.5" and 7.25". The shorter ones also seem slimmer, about the same size as a larger Dark-eyed Junco, which also vary in size. I see many birds side by side on the bathroom windowsill,

and most of them are crouching as they eat, so I am in a good position to compare sizes. I learned in one drawing class with John Muir Laws that birds are shapeshifters, capable of elongating their necks or puffing out feathers to stay warm, which makes them look obese or like babies. When they are on alert, the neck elongates. I watched one Golden in the water bowl tilt back its head and expand its whole body as it drank. Its throat was full and it appeared to be gargling.

I would know a lot more about Golden-crowned Sparrows if I went to their home turf in Alaska or northwestern Canada. Where do courtships happen and what are the rituals? I read that they mate for life, yet I have not seen any that look like a mated pair. They're not like California Towhees; when you see one towhee, you will soon see the other following it around. Do the male and female Golden-crowned Sparrows remain apart in their summer home and only reconnect up north to breed? Do both parents feed the young?

If the Goldens follow the same migration schedule as in previous years, they will be in full sexy regalia by the first or second week of April, and over the following week, they will head for the shrubby tundra that is so different from my Oak Woodland backyard. By then I will see a lot more than just fluff in the birdbaths. I will have to control my criminal impulses and not take those feathers into the house.

February 8, 2021

When I first started watching birds in my backyard, I read an article on feeders. There were many excellent points on how to choose feeders to match birds in the area and to keep out squirrels. The most interesting thing I learned was this: Feeders present an artificial situation for birds. Many kinds of birds will come to the same feeders at the same time, and they might be birds that don't normally hang out together in the wild, either with their own kind or with other species. That intermix for the same food makes it inevitable that there will be challenges and aggressive displays. That one bit of information has guided much of my observations. I have to bear in mind that the bird behaviors I see in my backyard may not be typical of what happens out of my viewing range.

The cages I built are like a stage set for seeing bird drama. I recently built a longer rectangular one, the size of two square cages. I set it on the ground so that the inexperienced ground feeder birds could more easily find their way inside. Most ground feeders were already skilled at this. I can tell a bird is a first-timer when it looks inside the cage but does not enter. I placed three bowls inside, all of them with crumbled suet, which all the ground feeders love. Soon, the suet bistro had many customers, Golden-crowned Sparrows, a California Towhee, two Spotted Towhees, a Bewick's Wren, a Dark-eyed Junco, and a White-throated Sparrow. Each bird took time to investigate the best side for entering the cage farther from competitors. As I noticed a while back, almost all the birds are deferential to the White-throated Sparrow and only one bird was not submissive: the California Towhee. It is bouncer-sized.

Although both California and Spotted Towhees have in the past gone into the cages, this California Towhee was uncertain how to fit itself through one of the wire grid's 1.5" square openings. The towhee eyed the food and circled all sides of the cage. It squeezed its head and shoulders through one opening, but could not squeeze past its breast. It backed out fast. It went to another side and did the same. A Golden-crowned Sparrow stood nearby waiting its turn, but backed away when it saw a White-throated Sparrow. I thought the towhee would give up. But then it saw the White-throated Sparrow hop in, grab some suet, and hop out. The towhee immediately did the same, as if it were the same size as the White-throated, clearing the wire opening without touching it. How did the White-throated give the substantially larger towhee the idea that it, too, could fit in? Does the towhee have a sense of its comparative size? How did the towhee make itself smaller so quickly? The only answer I can think of: Birds are magical creatures and this was one of its magic tricks.

PERCHERS AND GROUND FEEDERS

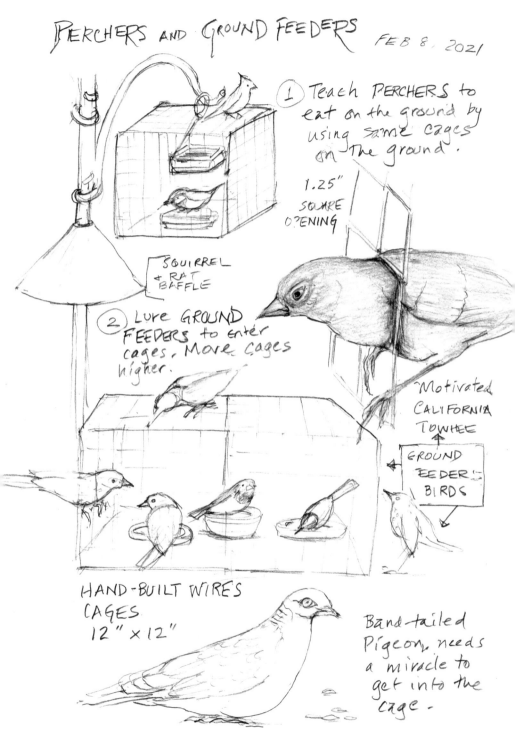

1. Teach PERCHERS to eat on the ground by using same cages on the ground.

1.25" SQUARE OPENING

SQUIRREL + RAT BAFFLE

2. Lure GROUND FEEDERS to enter cages. Move cages higher.

Motivated CALIFORNIA TOWHEE

GROUND FEEDER BIRDS

HAND-BUILT WIRES CAGES 12" × 12"

Band-tailed Pigeon, needs a miracle to get into the cage.

March 21, 2021

The other day, I saw a black and white cat in our yard. I immediately ran toward it shouting, and it took off.

The cat had been skulking near the fence and around the ivy, vines, and bushes. That's where a pair of Spotted Towhees hang out. The next day, a Spotted Towhee limp-hopped out of the bush into view. It was the smaller, less vibrantly colored of the two, the female of the mated pair. Her right foot was gone, and the remaining part of her leg was freshly shredded, dangling uselessly. I suspected the cat I saw had something to do with this. The remnant of leg dragged behind her and got caught on the lip of a water bowl. Later it caught the edge of a rock. Would the male Spotted Towhee stay with its disabled mate?

I am afraid this will eventually prove to be a mortal injury. It seems to me that a missing foot and useless leg decreases its chances of survival. A hawk would take a slow bird. Because it is a ground feeder, it needs to hop fast, jump, and kick back dirt. This female is no longer able to make quick springy hops. Is there a chance it will eventually learn to move more adeptly? Will the shredded leg become infected? I wish I could catch it and take it to WildCare, so it could have that useless dangling piece of leg removed.

It drives me crazy when I hear cat owners tout pseudo-scientific statements, like this one: "Cats are apex animals. Cats eat birds. Birds eat worms. That's nature taking its course. Get over it." My response: Coyotes and Great Horned Owls have more apex status than their roaming cats and can eat them to prove it.

SHOCK AND SADNESS.

SPOTTED TOWHEE
MISSING A FOOT

MORTAL
INJURY TO
LEG?

VICTIM OF
A CAT?

June 23, 2021

Trouble in paradise. There are three California Towhees who are in my backyard all day long. Two of them seem to be fighting several times throughout the day. When they sit on the rail at the edge of the patio, there is usually another towhee sitting slightly below on the back cushion of a chair. The Bickersons start off with loose wings hanging down, rapidly flapping them. This wing-flapping is quite different from what fledglings do to beg parents for food. It seems to be part of a ritual. One of them turns its back on the other. Another dances in a tight circle. Sometimes they get close in each other's face, before they both rise up all at once with feet upraised. I assumed at first this was aggression. I have seen other birds show aggression with loose wings as they approach in a low posture. My armchair conjecture was this: the two flapping towhees are males and the one watching is a female waiting to declare the victor her mate. But one expert birder I know said those behaviors were consistent with courtship between a male and female towhee. So who is the mystery third towhee watching all this flirtation that will lead to copulation? Maybe it's their offspring, a young male getting pointers on courtship? What did it learn?

CALIFORNIA TOWHEE
LOVE or WAR?

I've seen two Calif Towhees lower and flap wings whenever they are near each other. Sometimes a third towhee is nearby. This is not the wing or tail flutters that fledglings do for food from parents.

·turned back to other Towhee and raised one wing

Was it a sexy dance of courtship or a war dance over territory between males in front of a female? I am guessing the latter.

June 29, 2021

Culinary notes: I pride myself a bit too much on having the best food for wild bird guests. I would never serve dried mealworms instead of live! That's like giving your kid frozen broccoli instead of fresh organic. A juvenile California Towhee appreciated my thoughtfulness. It was hogging the cage feeder with live mealworms, downing the wrigglers in quick succession, eating unabated. The towhee was burning through mealworms fifteen or twenty at a time. When it polished off the rest of the mealworms, I decided it was time to forgo culinary pride and switch to dried mealworms. They are a lot cheaper for an equivalent number. But would the various songbirds still find my backyard just as enticing? Last year, when a thousand live mealworms in a metal bowl died in 100-degree heat, the little birds rejected them outright. Perhaps stiff bugs are irritating in a tiny bird's crop. Bigger birds, it turned out, are less fussy. The doves and Scrub Jays readily ate the dead black mealworms. They fought over them.

Today I set out dried mealworms. The songbirds poked through the dish then tossed the dried ones in the air to get to the bottom of things. I refilled the bowl. An adult towhee went in the cage, picked up a dried mealworm, and quickly dropped it. It picked up another and dropped it. It poked through the bowl. Finally, it ate a dried one, then a second and third. It held one in its beak and left the cage, then evidently it came to its senses, dropped the inferior mealworm, and headed to the birdbath for a prolonged splash and maybe to wash its mouth out. In the meantime, a juvenile towhee arrived on the patio where it hopped around looking for crumbs. It spotted the dried mealworm the adult towhee had abandoned. It picked it up and immediately swallowed it. I threw out more on the patio and it ate those up as well. Jubilation! I feel like a mother who got her kid to eat frozen broccoli.

July 14, 2021

On Sunday, Asa, one of my oldest, dearest friends, died of a massive heart attack. Over two days and sleepless nights, I thought about all we had experienced together over the last fifty-one years. Much of it was hilarious, like the time Asa dressed in drag to imitate me by wearing Issey Miyake clothes, toting two stuffed toy Yorkies in a purse, while singing custom lyrics to the tune of "Don't Cry for Me, Argentina."

Today, as I was looking out onto the patio, I saw the usual Dark-eyed Juncos pecking the ground for spillage, the Pygmy Nuthatches coming in pairs to raid the mealworm bowl and carry back food for their nestlings. A pair of California Towhees were doing aggressive wing displays to each other, eventually rising in mid-air with feet upraised. And then I saw an American Robin. It was sitting on top of the fence, looking kingly with its bill classically upraised. They are common enough in some habitats, but in my backyard, they are rare. I had seen one in my yard only three times in the last five years that I had been noticing birds.

A few minutes later, I saw a critter that had never visited our yard before. A chipmunk with vivid white and dark stripes that ran along its face and over its rich brown back. It was sitting on the upraised concrete planter that runs above the walkway, right under the Japanese andromeda bush, which was next to a tangle of jasmine vines—not exactly the forest habitat where one usually finds these chipmunks. In fact, I had never seen chipmunks anywhere in Marin County, nor had those I asked. A California Towhee flew to the barbecue grill and leaned forward, staring at the newcomer from about a foot away. The chipmunk did not flinch. It remained sitting on its haunches. After a minute, the towhee left, and the chipmunk slowly retreated into a thicket of vines.

JULY 14, 2021

The chipmunk was not fearful
in its manner when the towhee
approached. It simply sat still.
Ironically, I had always pictured
Asa as a towhee, which
I find to be comical
and lumbering
birds, a little
more curious
than other
birds in
exploring
what is
inside
the room
beyond
the glass.

Sonoma
chipmunk

I was still marveling over these two lucky sightings when a finch flew onto the feeder and sat on a metal ring. I assumed it was a male House Finch. They had recently returned, along with the ever-plentiful Lesser Goldfinches. But when I looked again, I saw the finch had a rosy tinge over the wings and no streaking on the flanks, breast, or belly. Its head sported a slight crest. It was a Purple Finch! This was another bird I had seen in my yard only a few times over the years.

All these sightings occurred within the same hour and should have remained simply a pleasant coincidence. However, I've long hoped in a wistful, wishful way that people I've loved and lost might return in some form to provide a better farewell. If the person came as a bird, it would have to be strikingly different to enable me to distinguish it from the usual avian crowd. And now, here I had had two unusual birds and a bonus chipmunk. The logical part of me reasons that there is no special meaning in this kind of randomness coinciding with grief and hope. Asa was an atheist who believed in science. He would have said that such notions were nonsense.

Many mutual friends would agree that Asa was larger than life, outrageous, dramatic, someone who made grand entrances, calling out in his barking voice that he had arrived and that we had to pay attention to him. If three critters are indeed a visitation, then this was overkill. And that, too, was Asa—over the top, excessive in every way. I can hear him yelling in exaggerated exasperation: "How many times do I have to get into animal drag for you to acknowledge it's really me?"

JULY 14, 2021

When the chipmunk appeared the California Towhee flew to the BBQ grill to check out the newcomer.

California Towhee

It leaned forward from about 12"-18" away. This can be an aggressive posture with birds, but the Towhee actually appeared curious. It had been flapping its wings and fighting another towhee just before.

July 15, 2021

The Showdown: In the right corner, enter the juvenile Scrub Jay, standing 11 inches, brazen, cocky, loud, clever, and always hungry. Its big strong bill is similar to its corvid cousin's, but was smaller than a full-grown adult's. When it comes to a food fight, the smart money is on the Scrub. The only time it fails to get to the food is when this human runs out shouting and waving her arms. In the left corner is an adult California Towhee, standing 9 inches, who does not seem particularly clever, but perhaps its clueless expression is subterfuge. When it comes to food, it is persistent. It has never met a live mealworm it does not like.

The jolly towhee bopped around the yard, eating suet in different cage feeders. Its crop must have been full to bursting, because instead of swallowing another nugget of suet, it dropped it on the patio. It was a fairly substantial chunk. The conniving juvenile Scrub Jay immediately swooped down, but before it could reach the morsel, the towhee rushed forward to face the interloper. Although the Scrub Jay is longer and heavier, the towhee got into an aggressive forward stance, as if to charge. Juvenile Scrub Jays are always hungry, but the posturing of the towhee had an effect. It did not move, either to advance or retreat. It watched the towhee grab the suet and gobble it down. The Scrub Jay youngster flew away.

I am aware I have committed the naturalist's sin of stereotyping the towhee as jolly and Scrub Jay as conniving. Science would require me to be objective and to not let personal bias obstruct more accurate observations. Thank God I am not a scientist. I love the jolly towhee and the smart and conniving Scrub Jay.

7-15-21

I'M A JUVIE! I'M HUNGRY!

I don't know other motivations, like how hungry the bird is or its babies.

But SIZE has usually been the winning deteriminant. NOT so, with this towhee and scrub jay. The towhee had the suet first, defended its claim!

SUET

YOUNG CALIFORNIA SCRUB JAY

It did some aggressive posturing, advancing toward the jay. The jay backed off. The towhee grabbed the suet. The jay flew off.

August 21, 2021

The wildfires are still raging, one after the other. During the last month, three new birds came to the backyard. The new birds, however, were likely not driven by the wildfires to come to my yard. They are juveniles, young birds who are learning their habitat, and by coming to my yard, they have come to the wrong place, although not far from the mark.

The first was a Western Meadowlark, a bird that I see in the open meadow of Fort Baker. My backyard lacks the open space for the operatic meadowlark, who is best heard in an arena. The second was a Black-headed Grosbeak, a bird I have seen in the scrubby open terrain of the Headlands. The third new bird was a Hermit Warbler, a bird that prefers dense forests. The juvenile coloration for all three birds made them a challenge to identify. I had seen adult versions of the Western Meadowlark and Black-headed Grosbeak, but had never seen a Hermit Warbler, although I recognized its bill as warbler-shaped. The adult Hermit Warbler has a vivid black throat. This young bird had a grayish throat and cap. I presented the bird to a Facebook Bird ID group, and my guess was confirmed. I am learning. I was then told by several that I was lucky to see this bird in my yard. One experienced birder said the Hermit Warbler would be a lifer for him, meaning the first of this species seen in his lifetime, and thus one that would be added to his list. The only list I keep is the one for my backyard. And right now, I confess I am feeling rather bird proud.

8.21.21

WESTERN MEADOWLARK
7.20.21

NEW BIRDS & WILDFIRES

New birds come to the
spa during wildfires,
and when air quality
is bad. They bathe &
drink, then fly onward.

not often
found in
lower
areas

8.16.21

IMMATURE BLACKHEADED
GROSBEAK

HERMIT WARBLER

8.21.21

Last
year's
wildfire
guests

FEET WERE
SCALY &
CRUSTED,
AS IF
PEELING

9.6.20

WHITE-BREASTED
NUTHATCH

BLUE
LEGS

8.17.20

HUTTON'S
VIREO

September 26, 2021

At 2:30 this afternoon, I heard a loud metallic crash and ran to the porch by my office. On the flagstone was a large juvenile Cooper's Hawk lying on its back between the metal trash pail and a metal stand that held three cage feeders. The feeders were swaying. No doubt the Cooper's had done a fast dive to pluck a songbird from its perch.

I was shaken to see this magnificent bird right before me. I spoke to it softly. *I'm sorry. I'm sorry. I'm sorry.* In the past, I had seen Cooper's Hawks at a distance through binoculars or with a camera cranked out to full digital zoom. I had also sketched them in my nature journal, so I would recognize them in the future and distinguish them from the smaller Sharp-shinned Hawks. The injured hawk was huge, it seemed to me, at least twenty inches long, which suggested it was a female. Up close, she was no longer a composite of field marks. She looked mythical. Her plumage was rich brown on the upper parts and head, and soft cream on the underparts, with teardrop markings on the breast. Her eyes were yellow—all field marks that pointed to her being a juvenile. Given the time of year, she was perhaps only three or four months old. A baby.

Being young and inexperienced, she may not have understood that the birds on those perches are in protective cages. She probably banged into a cage trying to catch an unwary bird. Or her wing might have snagged the strings of the seed net I had recently attached under the feeders to catch the mess. The feeders were three feet from windows on two sides, and the wingspan of a female Cooper's Hawk can be up to three feet. Although both windows had decals to prevent window strikes, Cooper's Hawks are notoriously fast when they dive, making it hard for them to suddenly veer away. This was the wrong place for a young hawk to go hunting.

Cooper's Hawk (juvenile)

Her yellow eyes were dilated, and her mouth was ajar, a sign of stress and pain. As I came to her, she made no effort to escape. A bad sign. But she was alert and watched me as I came close. I turned her over and lifted her in both arms. How strong and fragile she was, both hard and soft. I was carrying a magical creature. She was docile, likely in shock, and it did not occur to me until later that had she not been injured she could have sunk her talons into my arm and held fast until I could reach the closest ER to extricate them. I searched for a box that would fit her. All were too short, until I finally found a soft-sided dog carrier with mesh windows. It was 18 inches long, a little small but good enough. As I was easing her into the box, she broke loose and flew toward a mirrored wall a few feet away. Our two small dogs barked and went running toward her, and I yelled at the top of my lungs. They stopped. The hawk slid down, unable to fly. This time, she allowed me to place her in the carrier without a struggle. Once she was in, I quickly took a photo on my phone, then zipped up the carrier.

Within twenty minutes of her accident, she was at WildCare, Marin County's only wildlife rehab center. I learned she had a suspected luxated wrist, which is at the bend of a bird's wing. Because it was no longer in place, it caused wing droop. A broken bone would have been easier to treat. The staff at WildCare explained that even if she could fly again, her luxated wrist would probably prevent her from having sufficient wing control to catch a fleeing mouse or bird. She would again crash or she would starve from her inability to feed herself.

On first assessment, she also appeared to have neurological damage, either from the collision, or from a previous accident or even an ingested toxin, like rat poison. Any of those things would account for why she miscalculated her dive. And she was underweight, a sign that she had not been a successful hunter. She had likely been on a path to starvation and would have joined the 75 to 85 percent of young raptors that die before reaching adulthood. I hoped she would still be among the 15 to 25 percent who would survive and fly for another twenty years. I imagined her sitting in our tree, her plumage turning gray and her eyes changing to red as she grew into adulthood. I imagined us looking at each other again many times.

Update: WildCare did rehab for two months and then transferred her to a larger aviary at a rehab center in Petaluma, where she had more room to fly. I received updates weekly. She gained weight eating frozen mice. We nicknamed her Miss Feisty because she did not tolerate being around people. She was tested regularly to determine if she could fly well enough to catch live prey. I was hopeful that I would be the one to release her in our yard.

She received a total of three months of incredible care. But she was still not flying symmetrically. A few days after that report, I received a voicemail message from the medical director, asking that I return her call. I knew by her soft, consoling tone that the news would not be good. I spared her the difficulty of telling me and left a voicemail message, saying I appreciated all that they had done. I knew that if Miss Feisty could not fly well enough to catch food, she would slowly starve in the wild. We knew by her disposition that she was not suitable to be an ambassador bird for their kids' programs. I understood why it was more humane to euthanize her, and I was grateful that they would do so in the kindest way possible.

After I left the message, I cried. I tried to draw her portrait. But I could not capture her spirit. I could not capture the way she must have felt when I briefly held her in my arms and told her I was sorry.

October 24, 2021

A bomb cyclone arrived in the Bay Area. It hurled serial storms and produced an atmospheric river that dropped a thirty-minute deluge. We, the denizens who had been saving shower water to wash bird poop off the porch, were happy to be waterlogged. Our cisterns were being filled. But as I watched the large limbs of our oak trees swaying, I imagined the birds in those trees being whipsawed and flung into the storm. Where do they go to stay dry when the rain is blasting sideways?

As if in answer, two Pygmy Nuthatches flew into the covered porch off my office, shook themselves off, and sat on top of a cage feeder a couple of inches apart. Most people would agree that the Pygmy Nuthatch is one of the cutest birds on earth. They look and sound like squeaky toys. I assumed they would eat a few suet balls for fortitude and head for a heavily leafed hiding spot. But after five minutes, they were still there. They did not budge when a sodden Scrub Jay dropped onto the rail and stared at me with a look of misery. Its bright blue feathers were so wet they were black and useless for insulating it from the cold. The bony shape of its skull was visible. In another second, it took off into the blustering rain, and I worried that it would die of exposure.

The Pygmy Nuthatches remained dry and unruffled. They did not go into the feeders to eat. They simply watched the rain from their spectator seats. The smaller nuthatch scooted closer to the bigger one. The bigger one then allopreened the little one, poking and picking at its feathers. I assumed they were adults, a mated pair, since the season for fledglings was long over. For thirty minutes, the two little nuthatches hunched close together like lovers on a porch swing, watching the rain as I watched them.

PYGMY PORT IN A STORM

Where do birds go in big storms. The bomb cyclone blew so hard that birds in trees were likely getting soaked. A Scrub Jay flew onto the porch, drenched, its feathers black — with no reflection in its blue feathers. Two pygmy Nuthatches settled on top of the feeder on the office porch. A mated pair? The smaller one scooted next to the other, who groomed the mate of mites and or other pests. They stayed side-by-side for 30 minutes watching the storm.

November 30, 2021

Whenever a female hummingbird drinks from the nectar feeder without being immediately chased off by a male, I suspect courtship has begun. To this human, it looks like the males are kinder. But *kinder* is a human trait and may not apply to birds. It would probably be more accurate to describe them as tolerant because they are motivated to get closer to the female and pass along their superior genes.

This female was still on the feeder when a male with a bright red hood and flashy gorget arrived. It buzzed around the female and came within inches of her. He did some air dance loop-dee-loops, and at first she showed no sign of being either receptive or rejecting. They clicked loudly while ascending and circling each other, until the male did his solo fireworks finale. I could not see how high he went, but in a typical courtship display, the male rises fifty to a hundred feet and does a deep dive in front of the female, culminating the show with a loud chirp-pop, the result of air being pushed through the outer tail feathers. Alas, the female was not impressed. *Ho hum, I've seen it before, only better.* If he had won her over, copulation would have taken four seconds—they are fast birds, after all—and the next second, this charming lothario would go off cruising for another female. He would not help build the nest, nor feed her or the nestlings. When I learned that the female does all the work, my appreciation increased exponentially. In most art photos and illustrations of hummingbirds, the males are depicted. They are more colorful. They sing. They do displays. The less flamboyant females receive short shrift, barely a nod to their existence, unless the photos include nestlings. Today I will start drawing a detailed portrait of a female hummingbird. I will think about all she does to ensure the survival of the feckless father's offspring.

ANNA'S HUMMINGBIRDS NOV 30, 2021

Has early nesting begun? Some do start
in early December, or earlier. I
saw a lot of
activity at the feeder.
A hummingbird was at the
feeder and an male
arrived. Instead of chasing
it off, It stayed to buzz
around. Several times it
came quite close and

female

yet the female was
not deterred from
remaining

MALE

Eventually, the male
and female rose up together.
There was much clicking. The
difference between the horizontal
chase and ascension —straight up—
must indicate some intent in this
behavior. My guess: early courtship

Oak Titmouse (fledgling)

Chestnut-backed Chickadee

White-crowned Sparrow (immature)

AMY TAN

SONG SPARROW

Song Sparrow

Great Horned Owl (female)

DARK-EYED
JUNCO

Dark-eyed Junco

Lesser Goldfinch

Dark-eyed Junco

Dark-eyed Junco (fledgling)

Oak Titmouse

January 8, 2022

The birds see me every day. I am their patron of good eats. They are unperturbed if I sit at the dining table inside and watch them eat, bathe, and cavort on the patio. They don't mind if I stand still next to the cage feeders and fill the bowls. But when I pick up the binoculars, even from a distance or from inside the house, the birds fly off. When I put down my binoculars, they usually return within twenty seconds. *Oh, it's just that flightless creature who brings the food.*

I took a photo of myself looking through binoculars and discovered I am VERY SCARY. I have big shiny dark eyes, like an owl's.

I am always curious how birds accommodate humans in their space. What is needed to dampen fright and flight? Mealworms and suet are not enough. I have thought about this notion of trust and fear in wild birds for several years. How could it possibly know that the large flightless creature will not grow hungry and eat it? What factors must be in place for a bird to trust me? Consistently bringing food. Staying my distance and letting them come to me. Not moving. I've made great progress. They are less wary.

I remind myself that I must be careful not to use terms that describe human emotions, like *trust*. But anthropomorphic paradigms are a start for looking at equivalents from a bird's perspective. I parse out the traits of human emotions to see if any are found in the behavior of birds. What about the two Pygmy Nuthatches that sat side by side watching the storm, while the male groomed the female by pulling off mites? Was that an avian expression of love? Do humans express it any better? Would Lou pluck parasites off my scalp and eat them?

PERSPECTIVE
PREY & PREDATOR
JAN 8, 2022

1-8-22

WHAT I SEE:
BINOCULARS,
BIRDS,,
   FLOATERS

SOMEDAY,
GOING TO
GET 10 × 42

MY
STARE

WHAT
BIRDS
SEE:
OWL EYES
= DEATH

WHENEVER I PICK UP THE BINOCULARS
AND AIM THEM AT A BIRD OUTSIDE,
THEY FLY OFF. I SUPPOSE I LOOK
LIKE I AM PART OWL, BUT HOW
IS IT THE BIRDS CAN SEE THRU GLASS
                              DOORS?

January 14, 2022

When I first read Bernd Heinrich's book *The Mind of a Raven,* I was tempted to cultivate a relationship with a crow. I imagined it coming at regular times, and our having crow-human exchanges. It might even imitate a few words and bring me gifts. The crows, however, did not come singly to our yard. They arrived as a clan, ten to fifty of them, often shrieking in histrionic agitation over who knows what. I later shifted the fantasy of bird buddies to another corvid, a Scrub Jay, one of the first birds I identified in my yard. They usually come to the yard one at a time, emitting a few loud squawks, which often draw the attention of one or two other jays that chase away the first.

I have since discarded the notion of a bird-human friendship. I love that the birds are wild, but my relationship with the Scrub Jays is complicated. They scare away the smaller birds by landing like a bomb and devour their food. I managed to get rid of the squirrels by switching to hot pepper suet. But the Scrub Jay proved to be a more clever opponent. I bought a square feeder with plastic sides. The opening closed when a bird heavier than an ounce landed on it. A Scrub Jay weighs 2.8 ounces. However, the jay found a way to cling to some portion of the outer cover so that it was nearly weightless for a second or two, which was enough time to grab a bunch of seeds. None of the store-bought feeders kept the jays or squirrels out, and I resorted to building my own feeders out of panels of wire grid that are used to build flimsy shelves. Those worked great. The little birds went in. The Scrub Jay clung to the sides and watched.

But now the Scrub Jay has developed new problem-solving skills that prove it is the smartest bird on the block. When the huge weeklong rainstorms came, I took the feeders down and placed them on a table under a patio umbrella. Soon I saw a Scrub Jay sitting on the

PROBLEM-SOLVING   JAN 14, 2022

The Scrub Jays display three methods for breaking into the cage feeder. #1 Grab the branch that blocks him from reaching the suet. #2 STICK bill in and grab on to bowl and slide it forward. #3 STICK whole head inside. No fear? It cannot extract head quickly.

SEQUENCE OF PROBLEM-SOLVING

2

#1 REMOVE BRANCH STUCK IN CAGE

GUILLOTINE METHOD

GRAB LIP OF BOWL AND DRAG TOWARD HIM.

3

STICK WHOLE HEAD IN!

table, now able to easily stick its bill in and nab food in a plastic bowl that was set a little too close to the corners. Easily fixed. I put all the food in a glass bowl and set that in the center. The Scrub extended its bill through the grid openings, far enough in that it could push the bowl closer to the other end. It would then go to that end and pull the glass bowl toward it and eat at its leisure. I set the bowl on a white silicone pad to keep it from sliding. The next morning, silicone confetti littered the table and flagstone, and the empty bowl was next to the side of the cage. I laced branches through the sides of the cages to keep the jay from poking its bill inside. The Scrub pulled out the branches. That was a new one. I stuck stronger sticks through the grate. By morning they lay on the ground, some of them pecked in two. I added tall rocks surrounding the bowl, and by morning, I saw the Scrub had pushed them aside. I put bricks on four sides. Those were immovable. I win!

Then I saw the Scrub Jay stick its entire head in the cage, guillotine style. It ate leisurely at Marie Antoinette's Bistro. The Scrub was vulnerable to attack from behind. A big towhee could enter the cage from the other side and attack the Scrub's face. Its tolerance for danger was impressive.

Were these break-in behaviors the work of one genius bird? Are they behaviors newly acquired by trial and error to fit the puzzle I had created? More likely, the Scrub Jay already possessed the same or similar problem-solving skills that it used in the wild. Pulling food out of crevices for example. Tearing acorns off branches. Pushing aside obstacles. I'm guessing it simply combined whichever skills it already had to solve the puzzle at hand.

I give kudos to Scrub Jays for their ingenuity and persistence. I too am persistent. I tried a kinder approach: a large nut-encrusted cone of suet, just for Scrub Jays, hung on the other side of the house, away from the songbird feeders. They haven't touched it. Too easy.

January 21, 2022

Lou told me there was a dead squirrel on the pathway going down to the lower garden. Fresh entrails were strewn about and the body of the unfortunate creature was missing its head. Lou assumed he had interrupted the animal that had killed it, probably a Red-tailed Hawk or maybe even a Great Horned Owl. We have seen Red-tailed Hawks land in our trees only twice. And while we have heard Great Horned Owls a dozen or so times over the years, usually at dusk or calling like ghosts in the darkness, we had never seen one in the yard. But today, I heard one call out at about 3 p.m. while I was refilling the bird feeders. Its call is unlike any other owl's, a strong, steady, single-pitched *Hoo-hoo. Hoo. Hoo.* Some mistake the soft gurgling coo of a Mourning Dove for a Great Horned Owl. But the dove's call is not evenly pitched. The second note rises a fifth, which approximates in human musical tones A E A A. The owl's single-pitched call sounds like it is an octave lower: G-G G G. It is deeply sonorous and reverberates far and wide. Its voice is a saxophone, the dove's a recorder.

By coincidence, my nature journal mentor, eighteen-year-old Fiona Gillogly, and her mother, Beth, arrived for a visit on their way to Point Reyes. Fiona, of course, was eager to see the carcass. She immediately identified it as a baby opossum, not a squirrel. She pointed to the bare tail that makes people mistake this marsupial for a rat. We then found the opossum's head. I love opossums, but I know raptors must eat, especially the young ones learning to hunt. The opossum's innards were turned inside out, revealing the spine—the classic dining habits of a Great Horned Owl, Fiona said. I later read that the head is especially favored for the eyes and brain, which may have already been scooped out.

At dusk, as I was working at the dining room table, I saw a huge bird fly out of the darkening stand of oak trees. It streamed by the verandah, a blur against a fading sky and bay waters. I rushed to the window at the other end of the room and saw the large bird enter the leafy shadows of an oak tree in our front yard. It was masked behind a tangle of branches and clusters of leaves. But then I saw another dark figure in the same oak tree, perched in the crook of a large limb, the silhouette of a huge bird with ears, the quintessential shape of a Great Horned Owl. In a few seconds, the owl hidden in the shadows flew out of the tree and the owl on the limb followed it to a distant tree.

It is nesting season for owls and these two might be a mated pair. I am hoping I will hear the screaming cries of perpetually hungry owl nestlings in the next two months. In the meantime, I must be vigilant to not let my four-pound dog suffer the grim fate of the baby opossum.

JAN 21, 2022
5:15 PM

♫ ♪ ♪
HOO-HOO HOO HOO

Songs of
Dusk

In the afternoon,
while filling the
bird feeders. I heard an unmistakable
Hoo-Hoo. Hoo Hoo. A Great Horned Owl.
I had heard them numerous times & saw
evidence of their presence — severed baby
opposum's head and body eviscerated,
inside out, which Fiona said was classic.

OWLS
are
NESTING!

At dusk, I saw a
large bird fly by
the window where I
was working. I
ran to the back
window and saw a
huge owl in the
crook of the oak
tree. The other owl
was hidden — but then
it appeared and flew
off and the owl in
the tree flew off
with it!

February 4, 2022

Our cistern full of rainwater and runoff from the roof had to be drained due to a failed pump and clogs caused by years of leaves and debris. 4,500 gallons of water were released into a large drainpipe, which sent water gushing down a retaining wall.

Many birds immediately flew over to see this novelty. They are always attracted to gurgling water. To our surprise, a California Towhee jumped onto the sloped retaining wall and rode down what was effectively a waterslide. It jumped off at the end of the short ride and then returned to the top of the wall to do it again. This was astounding. Other towhees waited their turn. Some birds sat in the bushes by the waterslide, watching the slalom event. Farther below, the gutters in the lane were flowing and the drain was bubbling over. The Golden-crowned Sparrows jumped onto the water and flapped about. It reminded me of city kids in the summer running through the spray of a broken fire hydrant. What is it about gushing water that excites birds and kids? I felt the same way when I was six. There was nothing better than a lawn sprinkler on a hot day. It was play, without any purpose, except to have fun and scream.

So what's play to a bird? I wondered about this when I saw birds using the swing suspended from a shepherd's hook. It seems to be behavior that does not serve any purpose, not any I can see—neither to find food nor to show aggression, for example. The behavior has much to do with instability, balance, and repeated movement. When they use a swing, is it like the sensation of being on a branch swaying in the wind? Is it a display of prowess? Does the pleasure in doing it require other birds to watch? What about waterslides? Is there a counterpart in nature? The birds in my yard don't swim, and they avoid water of an unknown depth. But maybe the towhee jumped on thinking it was a shallow birdbath and then found itself sliding? There was no danger.

Playfulness in Birds

waiting for a turn

Because of water contamination, we had to drain the cistern, which holds 5500 gallons of water. A drain pipe funneled the water over the edge of the patio and created a waterfall.

This attracted many birds, and several towhees jumped onto the water-slide flowing down a concrete retaining wall. Other towhees waited their turn. The drain at the bottom in the lane was clogged and three Golden-crowned sparrow jumped into the fountain — like kids around a broken fire hydrant

It only had to jump off. Perhaps these activities are to practice skills that improve strength and performance, and the practice itself happens to be enjoyable. Humans do that, be they acrobats, surfers, skiers, or skydivers. These questions beg other questions. Why did the birds take turns with a novelty? Birds often avoid newness. Why were the other birds interested in taking a turn? It seems that the successful demonstration by the first towhee was good enough to deem it safe.

If birds play, what about amphibians and fish, bees and butterflies, spiders and ants? Is there a phylogenetic line that limits playfulness to birds and mammals? What is the purpose of play? What's fun to a bird?

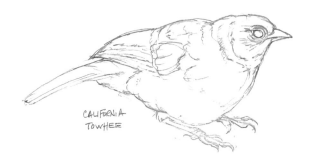

CALIFORNIA
TOWHEE

February 28, 2022

Birdwatching is disruptive to Zoom meetings. One time, I jumped out of my chair and yelled, "Purple Finch!" Fortunately, the people at the meeting were nature lovers. Today, during a Zoom call, I kept the audio and video turned off and kept my binoculars on the table so I could tune in to any unusual activity, like the young Golden-crowned Sparrow that was hopping slowly across the patio. Its pace was unusual. I looked through the binoculars. It was missing its left foot and part of its leg. Whenever I see sick or injured birds, I feel sympathetic pain. With this bird, I imagined the many ways it could have lost its leg, the frightening circumstances—caught by a snap trap or glue trap, wedged into the deep elbow of two limbs, snatched by a predator, like a cat, tangled in fishing line, torn off on barbed wire, or lacerated by thorns in a blackberry bush.

I posted on a Facebook page for birders, describing the wound. One person assured me that one-legged birds easily adapt and can live as long as two-legged birds, no problem. Was that sunny prediction based on anecdotal evidence that pertains to pet birds? Does it apply to resident birds whose territory is a radius no bigger than a backyard with a dozen feeders providing copious amounts of food? Would it apply to birds that migrate to Alaska? Has anyone followed one-legged migratory birds for a year to see if they survive?

I am a worrier. The one-legged Golden-crowned Sparrow is a migratory bird. In a little over a month, it must fly thousands of miles to reach its summer home. It will need to hunt along the way. With only one leg, can it scratch dirt deep enough to uncover worms and insects? Will it be less adept at perching to forage for berries and seeds? As a less efficient hunter, it may become underweight, and without reserves to complete its flight home, it will fall out of the sky. I can picture it.

As if to confirm my worries were well placed, I saw the Golden-crowned struggle to hop onto a terra-cotta saucer and remain balanced so it could dip its head and drink. It fell off. It had not adapted. I sense the bird was doomed. Its plumage suggested it was a young bird, and statistics foretell a grim future. It would likely be among the 70 percent of songbirds that don't live to adulthood. The reasons are many, from predation by hawks, window collisions, cats, toxins, and starvation to disease and disability, like an amputated leg. If only this bird could overcome its homing instinct to fly north to the tundras and instead stay in my backyard, where food and water are plentiful, where a human will watch over it and never assume it will do just fine.

For birds, each day is a chance to survive.

2-28-22

Young GOLDEN-
CROWNED
SPARROW
missing a
leg. It
will have
to
migrate
in another
month or
so.

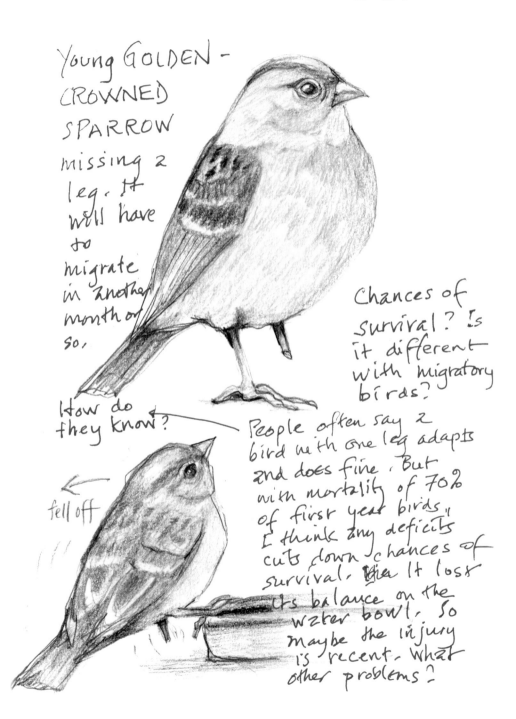

Chances of
survival? Is
it different
with migratory
birds?

How do
they know?

fell off

People often say a
bird with one leg adapts
and does fine. But
with mortality of 70%
of first year birds,
I think any deficits
cuts down chances of
survival. She It lost
its balance on the
water bowl. So
maybe the injury
is recent. What
other problems?

March 19, 2022

I put up a nesting box three years ago and nailed it to an oak tree. Beth and Fiona told me the nest box location was ideal: seven feet up, out of view of walkways, and within three feet of the lower branches of a tenacious old fuchsia tree. It's actually a shrub that looks like a tree, *Fuchsia paniculata,* which can grow to be twenty-four feet tall. Ours is tall and also spreads out to over twenty feet in misshapen diameter, and its branches have sent out so many twiggy tentacles they are like jungle vines that could pull a fence down or injure an inattentive person who walks into its many low-lying limbs—both of which have nearly happened, leading us to severely prune the megashrub. Its tangle of thick and thin leafy branches also makes it excellent camouflage for baby birds.

The nesting season coincides with spring, when the branches are heavy with panicles of pink flowers. The lucky bird that moves into the nesting box will have full amenities. A foyer, a.k.a. perch on a branch three feet from the nesting box, which enables it to assess its surroundings before taking a straight shot into the nursery. A playground, a.k.a. leafy spread that will give the future fledglings shelter from the elements and a safe harbor for hiding and moving about the yard. Fresh food, a.k.a. berries and nectar-laden flowers that attract nutritious insects. And privileges to a community center, a.k.a., oak trees visited by many birds and where crevices crawling with caterpillars, spiders, and flying insects are easy to plunder.

Evidently the birds did not think the nest box was that hot a deal. For three years, I had no takers. The empty box mocked me. I told a birder friend that perhaps I should have set the box on a tall pole. Maybe birds are suspicious of boxes on a tree. Or maybe a rat was inside, living the good dry life with its hoard of bird food. Or maybe the box is creeping with mold.

I decided to inspect the box to see if anything was amiss. As soon as I opened it, an Oak Titmouse flew out. *Omigod! Success.* I quickly counted three eggs, shut the door, and left. I worried that the female would not return. She and the male were clearly agitated. They gave continuous streams of *tsika-tsika-tsika* curses before disappearing into the fuchsia shrub. I saw them inspecting all reaches of the front yard, hopping within the lower branches, as if I, the miscreant, might be hiding there. I had already retreated to the house and was watching from a window by the front door, about twenty-five feet from the nest box. A half hour later, the female positioned herself on the branch nearest the nesting box. After two false attempts, she slipped into the box. The male remained outside, hunting. He jumped from branch to branch, calling out *tsika-tsika-tsika.* I saw him next on top of a branch holding in its bill bright red caterpillars from an oak tree. And then he sang out a melodious tune, longer and more varied than the "Peter! Peter!" most birders describe as the titmouse's song. More astonishing, the female in the nest box returned a brief version of this song. While females do sing, few birders have heard them. This was definitely a bird-proud moment. She sounded plaintive—*I suffer alone in darkness for our future children.* Or maybe she was complaining: *Where's the frigging food?* The male flew to the branch near the nest box entry. He looked around the yard, then flew into the nest box with the meal for his mate.

I am calculating when I might expect to hear nestlings, and when I might see fledgling faces peeking out of the hole in the nesting box. Fiona Gillogly said that if there are only three eggs, it could be that the female is still laying eggs, an egg a day. Four total is typical. Hatch time would happen on a schedule based on the full nest. She could take another week before she finishes. And then we'll hope the squirrels or larger birds don't take the eggs for their supper.

I'm optimistic. It's time to go to the bird store to order live mealworms.

April 20, 2022

I am dreading what will happen any day now. Over the last month, the Golden-crowned Sparrows were spending much of their time bathing. Most of the adults have already changed into breeding plumage, while the first-winter, duller-colored birds have molted into aerodynamically smooth feathers. They have been eating constantly. I once asked someone in a bird group whether birds ever overeat and get fat. The gist of the answer was: No, their special regulated metabolism prevents them from becoming obese. I later read that migrating birds do indeed add a slight cushion of fat so they can survive the long flight home, but not so much that it would make flight more difficult. They arrive on the underweight side. I am learning I must be careful about information sources. How can anyone know everything about birds? Certainly no one should depend on me. I am all about free-form guesswork. That's the fiction side of me. I mull over all the possibilities, situations, needs, and intentions. Birds go by instinct and their own calendar of events, and whatever intentions they have in the moment are not shared with me.

One of the Golden-crowned Sparrows in breeding plumage looks obese, lacking a neck. It resembles a gray tennis ball with a sparrow's face plastered on it. It's not at all cold out, so it would not be puffed up to stay warm. Maybe its metabolism has gone haywire and it has become morbidly obese. How will it fly more than twenty feet at a time? I look at it again. It doesn't look sick. Who knows all the reasons birds puff themselves up?

How many days will they fly to reach home? I imagine how happy all the Golden-crowned Sparrows will be when they see thick clouds of monster mosquitoes clogging the air and larvae as big as mangoes hanging on every shrub.

The young Golden-crowned Sparrows in non-breeding plumage

left first. I wonder what kind of territory they would stake out that had not already been pre-reserved by the breeding bunch from last year. The breeding adults in my yard continued to feast and splash, growing more resplendent. Their thick black brows grew more intimidating, their yellow crowns more vivid. Each day there were fewer of them.

And now I see only one. It is poking around in the bushes. Will it follow instinct and fly thousands of miles home all alone? Or maybe it will join a band of other Golden-crowneds getting a late start. But if it inadvertently joins a different species of sparrows, or gets discombobulated, it could land in a strange place far from its northern tundra. It might even land in somebody's backyard in Calgary or Nova Scotia, where it would be the only one of its kind, a rare vagrant for a lucky bird lover.

FAREWELL TO
GOLDEN-
CROWNED
SPARROWS

Their favorite
has gone un-
touched

Bathing
frenzy
is
over

The last of the GCSP
have departed, and the
yard feels quiet, deserted.
The water saucers are un-
used, except for Spotted
Towhee who came by for a
bath in three saucers. The
Oak titmouse and Bewick's Wren
came often to the worm feeder,
which they were excited to see
contained live mealworms. They
came every few minutes.

April 25, 2022

From the dining table, I watched a young crow gathering acorns in the tree above the patio. It used its beak to grab on to a long pliable twig holding a few acorns, then twisted and yanked the woody shoot. I saw it swing down so that it was upside down, still hanging on to the twig with one foot. It bounced. How clever to use body weight to separate the acorn from the twig. But I soon realized it was not a strategy but a bad situation. It could not extricate its foot from the evil carnivorous twig. Luckily, persistence is one of the crow's many strengths, and after more jerking, it tore its foot away from the demon twig without tearing off its foot. I wonder how many other birds have lost a leg this way. The same crow jumped onto a steeply pitched branch. It slipped down jerkily and with an upheaval of wings it avoided falling off. The young crow inspected the tree bark, as if it had slipped due to a defect on the evil branch. This unsympathetic human laughed out loud. I once saw a young monkey in a zoo careening in a cage until it missed a rung and crashed to the floor. The humans laughed, and the monkey repeated the same mishap—missing the same rung—as if to prove that it meant to do this pratfall. Bruised ego, bruised body. Would a young crow have the cognitive ability to suggest a fake cause-and-effect to mask its embarrassment over its clumsiness? *It almost murdered me.*

What kind of cognitive skills would a crow possess to experience embarrassment? Self-awareness of recent behavior? Does embarrassment occur only with an audience? Does it know what it means when a human laughs at it? Would it overcome embarrassment by dropping poop on this human's head?

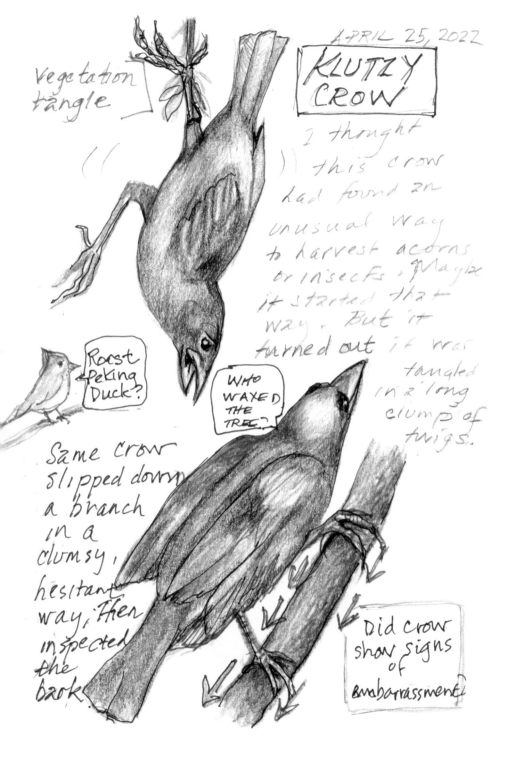

July 6, 2022

I am in danger of becoming even more obnoxiously bird proud. Several experienced birders told me they had never seen a Bewick's Wren bathing in water. These birders are the kind who get up at dawn's early light every day to see the night owl return to its roost and to hear the robins start the dawn chorus. A Bewick's is a common bird, and that suggests that the behavior has not been seen because Bewick's don't bathe, at least not in water. Someone said she had witnessed the bird dry-bathing, that is, lying prone in dry dirt to rub its body and flap its wings. I have seen other birds do that, but not a Bewick's.

From what I understand, bathing is an imperative for birds to maintain the flight-worthiness of their feathers, to help them molt, as well as to cleanse themselves of parasites, bacteria, and such. That's why I have many terra-cotta saucers on the patio. They are often used.

Three days ago, I looked up from the dining table where I work and caught sight of a young Bewick's Wren hopping along the three-foot-high wall of stacked rock. It might have been the same Bewick's that fledged a couple of weeks ago, a fluff ball that I saw begging its mother for food. This juvenile was sleek in appearance, but still visibly young in its indiscriminate curiosity over food. Of equal interest: safflower seeds and the seed-sized poop of the Golden-crowned Sparrows. It jumped off the low rock wall and onto the flagstone, then spied a muddy puddle about a foot in diameter. It was the dirty water that had not drained after I cleaned the water bowls. The little wren hopped over to it and drank. Ack! Clearly, it needed a lesson on what not to eat or drink. The young Bewick's then plopped its body into the poopy puddle and went into paroxysms of joyful splashing. It was bathing! It tried to dip its head into the water, but the puddle was too shallow. The Bewick's then got out of the puddle and shook itself. Just

BEWICK'S WREN BATHING!

I've heard many say they have never seen a Bewick's Wren bathing. Did they do only dust bathing? Today, a fledge tried to bath. It perched on the terra-cotta saucer then fell in.

Earlier, it splashed in a muddy puddle. It perched on a twig and groomed itself. But it slipped off three times.

when I thought I had witnessed the end of this funny bit of serendipity, the young bird flew up to the top of the rock wall and over to a terra-cotta saucer with clean water. It hopped up and perched on the lip. Had it done this before? It looked at the water, perhaps to assess its depth. And then it slipped and fell into the one-inch pool. It sat in the bath for a moment, perhaps surprised, and then splashed vigorously, cleaning itself of the dirty water from the puddle. I managed to get a photo of this historic event. After two minutes, it hopped onto the vine of the jasmine plant above the saucer. It shook its body head to toe, and poked its bill under a wing to groom—before slipping backward. Its toes were gripped to the vine and it was able to regain its upright position on the perch. I started taking video and captured it grooming and slipping again. It slipped a third time before calling it quits. The baby Bewick's Wren has come at least three times a day over the last three days.

I am not the kind to boast. So I waited a day before sending my birder friends the photos and video.

July 8, 2022

As usual, I was seated at the dining table, working. When I looked up, I noticed a House Finch flying back and forth in front of the glass door closest to me. At first, I assumed it saw its reflection as another bird, a competitor. But it did not attack the window, as most birds do to their mirror image. This bird was a female, not a territorial male. She kept flying back and forth, all the while looking at me. She landed on the window feeder, the plastic one that looks like a house. That feeder has perches for only two birds at a time. The birds act as if these perches are the equivalent to an 8 p.m. seating at a three-star Michelin restaurant. They squabble over the two perches. They jump on top of each other. There is always a line, as birds wait on the rail and in nearby trees. The feeder often runs empty of sunflower seeds, as was the case now. I had not bothered to refill it because the finches drop a lot of the seeds on the ground, and the mess attracts the rats that live in the ivy.

The female House Finch flew to a nearby large seed feeder that was full and sat in the mesh seed catcher. She continued to stare at me. *Twilight Zone* music begins. Mystical thoughts seep in. Is this the spirit of someone I know? The bird flew back to the empty window feeder, and resumed her frantic flying. Why? Could this bird possibly be signaling that I should refill its favorite feeder? I got a scoop of seeds and stepped outside. The House Finch flew about six feet away and sat on the rail. I poured in the seeds and left. The finch immediately went to the feeder and ate and ate and ate.

I have read many stories of intelligent birds that speak, understand language, solve puzzles, exchange gifts, complain about inedible food, express appreciation, show feats of sequential memory of tasks, and so forth. Humans tend to measure intelligence in animals based on whether their subjects can do what we do—speak, understand requests, create novel combinations of words into grammatical structures. Most of the subjects were domesticated birds, like parrots, or corvids, like crows or ravens. Scrub Jays can outsmart humans, as I can attest. But I've never read anything about the intelligence of House Finches—not that my search has been anything but catch-can and superficial. Has anyone ever devised a way to assess the specific forms of intelligence that a wild House Finch might have? In the bird universe, what counts as extra smart?

I now recall three instances when I removed feeders because of outbreaks of salmonellosis, conjunctivitis, or avian pox. Each time, there were birds that sat by a window and stared at me. Actually, they seemed to be glaring. A few of them gently tapped the window with their beaks. Two of them followed me from window to window. And on two occasions, the birds flew in as soon as I opened the door. They must have sensed that their food was inside the house.

People often talk about how smart birds are. Is it so far-fetched to think that a bird can do what my dog often does? If he wants to play fetch, he pats my leg and runs in the direction of his cabinet of toys, pausing to see if I understand and am following him. Didn't this House Finch do something similar? If a bird deliberately initiates interaction with a human, that's a pretty smart bird, in my opinion. If the bird persists in communicating something specific, like my need to refill its favorite feeder, that's a genius.

7-8-22

GENIUS BIRDS
vs
CLUELESS HUMAN
(ME)

A FEMALE
HOUSE FINCH
FLEW BACK
+ FORTH IN
FRONT OF
WINDOW WHERE
I SAT. WAS NOT
ATTACKING
HER
REFLECTION.
WAS STARING
AT ME

FEMALE
HOUSE
FINCH

TRAGICALLY
EMPTY

FULL SEED
FEEDER
SIX FEET
AWAY.

#1 ACRYLIC SEED FEEDER
ATTACHES WITH SUCTION CUPS,
HOLDS SUNFLOWER SEEDS.

I FILLED WINDOW FEEDER
AND HOUSE FINCH WATCHED
FROM THE RAIL. SHE
THEN ATE FROM THE
FEEDER AND NO LONGER
DID HER FRANTIC
FLYING.

SHE DID NOT EAT
SEEDS. JUST SAT ON
HOOP NET AND STARES
AT ME BEFORE FLYING
AGAIN IN FRONT OF
WINDOW FEEDER.

August 31, 2022

In mid-July, I heard the incessant shrieking of Scrub Jays. That invariably means they are mobbing a raptor in one of *their* oak trees. Scrub Jays have a broad sense of ownership when it comes to trees. They don't nest in ours. The oak trees are merely among the many way stations they use in their daily work as marauders and acorn foragers. Jack Gedney at Wild Birds Unlimited wrote about this. I paraphrase less elegantly: If each Scrub Jay caches thousands of acorns every year, over the last 150 years they've cached millions and millions of acorns in our town. Thanks to the Scrub Jays, our town is studded with oak trees on its hillsides as proof. So yes, these trees belong to the Scrub Jays by right of inheritance.

I scanned the oak tree and spotted a few Scrub Jays, noting the direction of their stares as a way to locate the offending raptor. There: a Great Horned Owl. *Omigod*. A rare deity in daylight. Invisible at night. I had not seen them since January, and it was only a blur of a bird flying by at dusk, shadows of two others. I gave thanks to the Scrub Jays for alerting me.

I heard the owl sing again, and then came an answer from another owl. It was at a higher pitch. I scanned the tree with my binoculars. I saw the second owl. It was bigger. I read that females are up to a third larger than males. Were these two a mated pair? The two owls took off and a few seconds later, I heard a loud shriek, which I mistook to be a cat being torn apart by the owls—until I later played a video of a juvenile owl screaming at its parents for food. I did some research. Adult males don't usually stay after the nesting season. They return when nesting starts again. That meant the smaller owl was not the male of a mated pair, but more likely the son of the larger owl, the mother. He was around four or five months old. Mom and Junior, we started calling them.

They have now been in the tree above our patio for over a month. Until this year, I had rarely seen an owl in the wild, and now I see two every day, all day long. I watch them snoozing, preening, and staring down at the ivy where the rats live. I see them regurgitating pellets with the indigestible bones, skulls, feathers, and furry bits of whatever animals they ate. The rats rarely come to the patio now. When they do, they are young ones, likely orphans, and within days, they don't return, leaving me to suspect they were a midnight snack for the owls. When I go out to the patio to refill the feeders, I try to be quiet. But sometimes the dog inside barks through a crack in the door. And the owls turn their heads and look down with those huge yellow eyes. After a few seconds, they close their eyes again.

There are many things in my life that make me feel I am very, very lucky. I can now add a pair of owls living in my yard as among them.

Great Horned Owl (female)

September 20, 2022

Two Great Horned Owls have been roosting in our yard for the last two months, enabling me to observe them eight hours a day and make a series of startling and important scientific discoveries.

GREAT HORNED OWLS

RESTING FACE

SEXY FACE

HAPPY FACE

MOTHER LOVE FACE

HANGRY FACE

ATTACK HUMAN FACE

© AMY TAN

September 30, 2022

It was a warm day and we had all the glass doors pushed to the sides. Bobo and our houseguests called my attention to a bird that was fluttering somewhere near the windows by the grand piano. It had fallen behind the pillows lining the banquette. How long had it been there? It must have been tired because I was able to catch it quickly with my hands. I looked at it in the hollow of my hands. Its tiny black eyes were wide open, not dazed or half closed, as they might be with birds that have struck a window. Its beak was closed. Birds in stress tend to pant through an open mouth. I walked out to the verandah with our friends. I could now see more of its head. It was an immature Wilson's Warbler, only 4.75"—as small as a chickadee. I have seen this bird only twice in my yard, and both were adults with the classic solid black cap. If this little bird did not fly away quickly, I would then put it in what I call my "avian ER," a clear lettuce saver with perforated openings, stuffed with crumpled paper towels that formed a nest to keep an injured bird upright. I cover the box with a black cloth napkin and place the box on the heated radiant floor in the bathroom. This warbler was alert. I opened my hands like a clamshell. The warbler looked around. There were big oak trees to the left and right, a bamboo hedge in front, and smaller trees and shrubs all around. It made a dash for the small tree on the right, good choice, a favorite among the hummingbirds and smallest songbirds.

It is not unusual for birds to fly into the house when two sides of the room are almost completely open. The room becomes more an open pavilion. But because the birds don't always fly out immediately, I placed anti-collision decals at both ends, and added hand-drawn white spiderwebs top to bottom on the patio side. Since adding the spiderwebs, I have not had any window collisions. But they do come in when the doors are wide open. They go all fluttery with confusion

BIRD IN THE HOUSE: WILSON'S WARBLER

Warm day and the bifold doors were pushed all the way to the sides, leaving an opening of 20 feet on one side and 12 feet on another. A bird flew into our aviary. I thought it was a Lesser Goldfinch, a pretty common bird, but when I finally had the bird in my hand, I saw it was the delightful WILSON'S WARBLER!

I GOT STUCK BEHIND PILLOWS!

We heard fluttering but couldn't find the bird for a while. He was exhausted when we saw him behind pillows.

← LETTUCE SAVER

VENTED

AVIAN E.R.

ANTI-WINDOW STRIKE DRAWN SPIDER WEBS

If this had been a window strike, I would have put it in the AVIAN ER & taken it to WILDCARE.

once they breach the boundary between outside and inside. Some fly up to the skylight and then down toward a window, and those who have failed to exit usually wind up on a sill at the back of the room where they either flutter helplessly against the window or rest and look around. Some of them quickly see the exit, a 20-foot opening. But of those that get in trouble and need rescue, almost all have been juveniles. Like human adolescents, they seem to be curious about everything and less cautious. When they get into trouble, they are less able to extricate themselves.

Do the birds I've rescued look at me differently later? Am I viewed as less dangerous? Or in a bird's mind, am I the reason they got into trouble?

November 9, 2022

I am seeing a lot of what I can only describe as sudden politeness among some of the male birds. They no longer chase females away from the food. They allow them to feed, to be close by, to not be chased away or dive-bombed. Is this a courting behavior? But isn't it too early for that? Mating for most songbirds does not happen until March or April. Raptors and hummingbirds might begin in January.

When do other songbirds usually start courtship? Is it always close to the time when they mate? Do they pair-bond in late fall? Is this a mated pair from last year? Today, at the bathroom window, I threw down a half handful of sunflower chips, my routine each morning. A male Dark-eyed Junco is usually the first to arrive. When one comes, five will follow. For such a tiny, sweet-looking bird, they are surprisingly aggressive with their own kind and will chase away other juncos that dare land on the sill while they are busy stuffing themselves. They also look at me every few seconds. If I don't move, they will remain. Most of the other birds that visit the sill are larger than the junco— the Hermit Thrush, Golden-crowned Sparrow, and Fox Sparrow— and when they land, the junco usually flies into the camellia bush.

This time, a female junco landed at the far left side of the sill. I could tell it was a female because her head was gray and her back was a paler brown than the male's. It was also smaller than the male, more slender, although perhaps the male looked bigger because he might have inflated himself a little, perhaps to appear more buff. The male hopped toward the female. At first, I thought this was going to be a typical challenge. But the female remained. When the male was a few inches away, it began bowing. It did this several times and the female watched. Then they both departed, flying upward in a spiral, similar to what male hummingbirds do when wooing a female. I was thrilled to witness this, what looked like courtship. Yet, why would they do this, when the nesting season would not begin until April or May? Mike Parr, president of American Bird Conservancy, told me that sometimes a bird will do courting behavior on a sunny day off-season. Spring is in the air—in December. I am guessing it will not lead to early mating. They are still dependent on food that is available in the spring, at least instinctively so. Eating at Amy's Bistro is not a wired instinct. I am also wondering how the female recognized that the approach of this male was not to chase her away? What signal did he show? Was it because he is already her mate?

I've heard that male juncos are excellent fathers. They help build the nest, feed the female when she is brooding, feed the nestlings, clean out the poop, and guide the fledglings as they learn to fly and forage. Does the mated pair stay together year-round? Did the male bow to tell his mate that they might start thinking about finding a new place to build a nest?

I'll be looking for other possible wooing gestures. Will he now allow her to eat seeds next to him on the sill? Will he bring her gifts of food, the equivalent of a diamond ring? The thought of this makes my heart sing. Will the male bird sing his heart out as well?

11/9/22

WHY ARE YOU BOWING? LAST WEEK YOU CHASED ME FROM FOOD!

I WAS YOUNG AND FOOLISH. I NOW WISH TO BE YOUR MATE FOR LIFE!

DARK-EYED JUNCO MALE is courting 4 months early. IS HE A CONFUSED IMMATURE?

THE JUNCOS IN OUR YARD USUALLY MATE IN MARCH OR APRIL AND THEN IN JULY. THIS MALE LIVES A LOT OF THE TIME IN THE CAMELLIA BUSH WHERE HE GUARDS FOOD FROM OTHER JUNCOS, INCLUDING FEMALES. BUT TODAY HE WAS ACTING ODDLY. HE APPROACHED THE FEMALE. SHE REMAINED, THEN WATCHED HIM BOW 3-4 TIMES. THEY THEN FLEW UPWARD IN A SPIRAL DANCE SIMILAR TO WHAT COURTING HUMMINGBIRDS DO.

December 2, 2022

Each morning, my husband and I look for Junior, the Great Horned Owl. His mother abandoned him in early October, and he now sleeps in one of two places, most often the spot closest to the patio, about twenty feet up. We happily accepted that he might stay for a while longer, months, years. Who knows? We enclosed two porches with wire screening, so we could let our little dogs outside without worry. The screen openings are still big enough for the songbirds to come in and visit the feeders.

Junior used to roost out in the open. But after his mother left, he is partially hidden. His body blends in amazingly well with the bark of the oak tree. I can spot him quickly, even without binoculars, only because he is typically on the same limb. If he is well-hidden elsewhere, I have to wait until he opens his vivid yellow eyes or turns his body and shows the white feathers on his face or chest. He is not disturbed by our presence. If I call, he might look, but usually he doesn't bother. He knows I am full of fake *hoos*. I no longer have to tiptoe around quietly when I am on the patio refilling feeders. Even when I am right below his roost, he doesn't blink an eye—meaning, he doesn't bother to open an eye to blink. Birds chatter; a squirrel once splayed on a limb to cool itself, not realizing at first it was right in front of the owl. The owl looked with some interest but decided he would rather sleep. Visiting kids talk to the owl. He looks but turns his head and goes back to sleep. So that's what we see from morning to dusk. At dusk, he sings for fifteen minutes before taking off when it is completely dark. Who did he sing to? Not a potential partner. He won't be mature enough to mate until next year at the earliest.

Two nights ago, at 2:40 a.m., I was awakened by the alarm of a car across the lane. I opened the door to the back porch to see whose car it was. Above the constant blare, I could hear two owls, a male's

Dec 2, 2022
1:45 PM

GREAT
HORNED
OWL

has taken up
residence in
our oak tree.

Remained or
our hours
sleeping

Rats have
declined in
population

On occasion, she
woke and looked at
me, the dog, and
maybe the rat we
saw.

deeper *hoo-hoo*ing followed by the female immediately singing back about four notes higher. They were engaged in excited conversation. Sometimes one owl interrupted the other, or sang at the same time. Was that courtship duetting? It was dark, so I could not see where they were, but considering I could hear them above the shrieking car alarm, they must have been close by, maybe even in the large oak next to the porch, where I briefly saw a pair of owls on two occasions last January. Weren't they bothered by the alarm? They were still animatedly talking to each other when I shut the door, and I did so only because I was freezing. Plus, the alarm was really annoying. My guess is that this was the mated pair that produced Junior. They probably would not mate until January or February. But I read that mated pairs, who stay together for life, might reunite earlier.

I am not counting on their building a nest in the same tree where Junior is. In any case, they would be too territorial to let Junior stay. Also, Great Horned Owls do not build nests or use nest boxes. They commandeer an existing raptor, corvid, or squirrel nest. I have never seen any of those in either our trees or those nearby. I have not heard the screaming of young raptors or corvids. Except for Junior's shriek when he flew after his mom to be fed, I have never heard other owlets crying, and they would be noisy enough for me to notice. Wherever they nest, my hope is that Mom will bring the fledglings to the same roost where she and Junior slept and preened and sometimes looked down at me, Lou, the dogs, and the little kids next door, all of us staring in awe at their yellow eyes and implacable faces.

December 6, 2022

I have spent so much time watching the winged action on my patio, verandah, and back porch that I have neglected to look up more often at what happens in the trees. But because I search for the owl each day, I do see other birds. Pygmy Nuthatches working in teams to cache sunflower seeds. An American Robin just under the canopy surveying where it will fly next. The Dark-eyed Juncos and Townsend's Warblers all bouncing around high in the oak tree.

Today, my search for the owl led to seeing a Nuttall's Woodpecker near where the owl usually sleeps. It had a spiky red cap, the signature adornment of a male Nuttall's. While I do occasionally see Nuttall's Woodpeckers going inside the cage feeders to eat the suet I plastered into the knotholes of a customized branch, I rarely see them in trees. They climb so fast, circling up a limb as if tracing the swirly lines of a candy cane. This Nuttall's remained still. Perhaps it was resting or sleeping. After twenty minutes, it got its motor running and jumped to different branches, which caught the attention of a Chestnut-backed Chickadee. The chickadee followed and watched from a discreet distance as the woodpecker pecked furiously into a branch for insects. When the woodpecker left, the chickadee went over immediately to examine what the woodpecker had dredged up, and probably to see if there were any leftover insects. Opportunistic foraging at its best. Had I not looked for the owl, I would have missed this.

Six years ago, I started watching birds knowing that feeders are an artificial situation that brings many species together at the same time and same place. I have seen territorial disputes between different species or within the same species. In the oak trees, however, the birds tend to be with their own kind and are in their particular branches in the tree. So perhaps there is less aggression up in the trees. If I looked up more often, I would likely see more courting behavior and cooperative caching of food in crevices. I might see mating. I would see species that do not come to feeders. I would see how Scrub Jays remove acorns, and possibly where birds are building nests. The downside would be a neckache from looking up for long periods of time.

In January, I will start a new journal. I will include much more of what I see in the trees, as well as on the ground where the sparrows and quail live and nest. I will sit outside on a low chair to watch the action on the ground. I will see where the sparrows and quail live and nest. I will see where the quail hide. That will require I remain frozen still, making no sound or twitch. To remain there motionless for an hour or so means I will also be frozen from cold. One must suffer for beauty, happily, for birds.

UP IN THE TREES

By looking at the feeders, I miss seeing life in the oak trees. I realized that when I searched for the owl and saw a Robin at the top.

I saw birds cacheing food in pairs.

I spotted a Nuttall's Woodpecker resting on a branch near where the owl usually perches.

When the wood-pecker roused, it jumped to a branch and began pecking. No doubt it was seeking insects beneath the bark. It dug in and soon left,

A chickadee went bounding over to see what the woodpecker was doing. It followed behind at a discreet distance, then flew to the place the woodpecker had been drilling. Leftovers?

December 15, 2022

If there is anything I have learned these past six years, it is this: Each bird is surprising and thrilling in its own way. But the most special is the bird that pauses when it is eating, looks and acknowledges I am there, then goes back to what it was doing.

Hermit Thrush

Orange-crowned Warbler

Gratitude

Many people unknowingly influenced the creation of this book. I cannot begin to describe all the ways you changed my life.

To my mentors: Bernd Heinrich, who showed me the importance of observing the same thing in the same place over many seasons; John Muir Laws, who taught me to draw, journal, and be intentionally curious in nature; and Fiona Gillogly, who freed me to wonder and wander in the woods and marshes like a child again.

To the biologists and ornithologists who did not think my questions were ridiculous, and instead found ways to help me further investigate: Bruce Beehler, Jack Dumbacher, Harry Greene, Lucia Jacobs, David Hillis, and Mark Moffett.

To the birders who took me into forests and to beaches, taught me birdsong, and patiently pointed to birds until I found them: Bob Atwood, Suzanne Badenhoop, John Baker, Jonathan Franzen, Joe Furman, Megan Gavin, Jack Gedney, Kathy Gervais, Keith Hansen, Mike Parr, Siddharth Dhanvant Shanghvi, Anne Stringfield, and David Wimpfheimer.

To the organizations who inspired my concern over the survival of birds and my involvement in bird conservation organizations: American Bird Conservancy, WildAid, WildCare, Point Blue Science and Conservation.

To members of the Nature Journal Club and Wild Wonder who

saw the early drawings and posts and provided encouragement. And to Beth Gillogly, for always including me in birding adventures and for the many opportunities, resources, and connections to people who helped me grow as a citizen scientist and artist.

To Caleb Statser, who worked long hours and dealt with technical challenges to turn piles and pages of drawings into images for the book.

To Marcia Soares and Abraham Perez, who recruited their children in ways essential to research: twelve-year-old Giovanni Perez, who filled the bird feeders and cleaned the birdbaths daily when I was away, and who also tromped through ivy and found the owl pellets. And to Liliane Perez, who sorted mealworms, dissected owl pellets, and enabled me to understand how mysterious and new everything in nature is to a five-year-old.

To my assistant, Ellen Moore, who read the early draft and heroically threaded the eyes of many needles to help me stitch this book together. You know the awful parts as well as the wonderful.

To the team at Knopf—Rob Shapiro, Andy Hughes, Rita Madrigal, Cassandra Pappas, and Jenny Carrow, whose support and enthusiasm for the book buoys me.

To my literary agent, Sandy Dijkstra. I am indebted to you forever for giving me the life of a writer, and for providing protection, counsel, and unbounded enthusiasm for whatever I do, which now includes drawing birds.

To my editor, Daniel Halpern, who gently nudged me to turn my scribbles and sketches into this book. You somehow understand what is in my work far better than I do.

To my husband, Lou DeMattei, who drove me to nature journal outings, classes, and birding locations and who never complained about the twenty thousand live mealworms stored in the fridge.

To all the birds in my backyard. If only you knew what I see in each of you. If only you knew how much I love you.

The Backyard Birds

These are birds identified in my yard as of December 15, 2022. Because band codes are sometimes used in handwritten notes, I include them here.

Corvids

American Crow (AMCR)
California Scrub Jay (CASJ)
Common Raven (CORA)
Steller's Jay (STJA)

Doves & Pigeons

Band-tailed Pigeon (BTPI)
Eurasian Collared-Dove (EUCD)
Mourning Dove (MODO)

Finches

American Goldfinch (AMGO)
House Finch (HOFI)

Lesser Goldfinch (LEGO)
Pine Siskin (PISI)
Purple Finch (PUFI)

Nuthatches

Pygmy Nuthatch (PYNU)
Red-breasted Nuthatch (RBNU)
White-breasted Nuthatch (WBNU)

Raptors

Cooper's Hawk (COHA)
Great Horned Owl (GHOW)
Red-tailed Hawk (RTHA)
Red-shouldered Hawk (RSHA)
Sharp-shinned Hawk (SSHA)
Turkey Vulture (TUVU)

Sparrows

American Tree Sparrow
(ATSP; rare vagrant in California)
California Towhee (CALT)
Dark-eyed Junco (DEJU)
Fox Sparrow (FOSP)
Golden-crowned Sparrow (GCSP)
Song Sparrow (SOSP)
Spotted Towhee (SPTO)
White-crowned Sparrow (WCSP)
White-throated Sparrow (WTSP)

Thrushes

American Robin (AMRO)
Hermit Thrush (HETH)
Varied Thrush (VATH)
Western Bluebird (WEBL)

Warblers

Hermit Warbler (HEWA)
Orange-crowned Warbler (OCWA)
Townsend's Warbler (TOWA)
Wilson's Warbler (WIWA)
Yellow-rumped Warbler (YRWA)

Woodpeckers

Acorn Woodpecker (ACWO)
Downy Woodpecker (DOWO)
Hairy Woodpecker (HAWO)
Northern Flicker (NOFL)
Nuttall's Woodpecker (NUWO)
Pileated Woodpecker (PIWO)

Other Songbirds

Anna's Hummingbird (ANHU)
Bewick's Wren (BEWR)
Black-headed Grosbeak (BFGR)
Black Phoebe (BLPH)
Brown Creeper (BRCR)
Bullock's Oriole (BUOR)

Bushtit (BUSH)
California Quail (CAQU)
Cedar Waxwing (CEDW)
Chestnut-backed Chickadee (CBCH)
European Starling (EUST)
Hutton's Vireo (HUVI)
Northern Rough-winged Swallow (NRWS)
Oak Titmouse (OATI)
Ruby-crowned Kinglet (RCKI)
Western Meadowlark (WEME)

A Selected Reading List

Here are some of the books I read and resources I used during the writing of this book.

Jennifer Ackerman
The Bird Way
The Genius of Birds

Jack Gedney
The Private Lives of Public Birds

Bernd Heinrich
The Homing Instinct
Life Everlasting
Mind of the Raven
The Nesting Season
One Wild Bird at a Time
A Year in the Maine Woods

Keith Hansen
Birds of Point Reyes
Birds of the Sierra Nevada

John Muir Laws

Laws Guide to Drawing Birds
Laws Guide to Nature Drawing and Journaling
San Francisco Bay Area Birds (set)
Sierra Birds: A Hiker's Guide
For an archive of free drawing classes:
www.JohnMuirLaws.com

David Sibley

Birding Basics
Birds West
What It's Like to Be a Bird

Apps
eBird
Merlin

A NOTE ABOUT THE AUTHOR

AMY TAN is the author of several novels, including *The Joy Luck Club* and *The Valley of Amazement,* as well two memoirs, *The Opposite of Fate* and *Where the Past Begins.*

She is a co-producer and co-screenwriter of the film adaptation of *The Joy Luck Club* and is the librettist for the opera *The Bonesetter's Daughter.* She received the National Humanities Medal, is a member of the American Academy of Arts and Letters, and serves on the board of American Bird Conservancy. She lives with her husband in Sausalito, California, and New York City.

A NOTE ON THE TYPE

This book was set in Janson, a typeface long thought to have been made by the Dutchman Anton Janson, who was a practicing typefounder in Leipzig during the years 1668–1687. However, it has been conclusively demonstrated that these types are actually the work of Nicholas Kis (1650–1702), a Hungarian, who most probably learned his trade from the master Dutch typefounder Dirk Voskens. The type is an excellent example of the influential and sturdy Dutch types that prevailed in England up to the time William Caslon (1692–1766) developed his own incomparable designs from them.

Composed by North Market Street Graphics,
Lancaster, Pennsylvania

Printed and bound by L.E.G.O. S.p.A., Italy

Designed by Cassandra J. Pappas